# CHE ELDER EDDA

# Che Elder Edda

Translated by
J. C. Buddemeyer

Northbooks
Eagle River, Alaska

Credits:  Rune fonts by Tesla Coil,

Digital Type Foundry, Seattle, Washington

Published by:

# ꓠORꜾꜾBOOKS

17050 N. Eagle River Loop #3

Eagle River, Alaska 99577

www.northbooks.com

in cooperation with Denali Institute of Northern Traditions

Chugiak, Alaska

Printed in the United States of America

ISBN 978-0-9720604-7-9

Library of Congress Control Number: 2009938604

# CONTENTS

The Elder Edda is not just a piece of Viking literature, it is a European masterpiece, and a world classic. It belongs alongside the other great works of antiquity. Like the Bhagavad-Gita, Tao-te-Ching, and the Christian Bible, the Elder Edda preserves the wisdom of our forefathers within a timeless framework of beautiful words.

With this translation, I have endeavored to present an accurate English edition especially tailored for dedicated students of Old Norse Literature. The text has been translated line by line (or half-line by half-line) in what I hope is the most meaningful interpretation possible. I have also retained a number of words which are significant concepts within the tradition. These terms are provided with definitions in the glossary, but the reader is encouraged to research them in other sources.

I have not included any commentary or footnotes because I wanted only to present the most useful translation possible, without distractions or extra opinions. Note, however, that the very act of translating these poems was an exercise in poetic license. I have tried to maintain literal accuracy, but in doing so I have lost the poetic beauty of the original. At times, the text may seem somewhat confusing with its archaic grammar and sentence structure, but I felt this was necessary to preserve the spirit of the original.

No translation of this sort can ever be perfect. I encourage the student who seeks something more to take the next step and become familiar with the original Norse text. It is my fondest desire that my work will inspire exactly this, and the student who does so will surely appreciate the line by line accuracy of this edition.

# ACKNOWLEDGMENTS

I would like to acknowledge the support I have received in bringing this work to life. My deepest appreciation to my brother, Adam , who painstakingly typeset, reviewed, and copyedited with me each line of poetry in this volume along with the many corrections as the manuscript evolved.

I would also like to thank Ragnar Holm of the Denali Institute of Northern Traditions in Alaska, my stimulus for scholarly investigation of the Northern Tradition, and who is also the co-owner of Northbooks, the publishing firm bringing this book to life in the literary world.

Without them both, this volume would never have seen  the light of day.

Thousands of years ago, migrating tribes of Indo-Europeans moved into northern Europe. They brought the same cultural and philosophical attributes common to all Indo-Europeans, but as time passed their civilization outgrew those early systems of thought. Their belief system became specialized and uniquely different.

Those beliefs manifested a tradition of complex poetry and song. Unlike their southern counterparts in Greece, the northern tribes did not commit these to writing. Instead, they relied upon memorization and oral transmission. It wasn't until the coming of Catholicism did anyone ever attempt to codify and record these "myths" of the North.

In the thirteenth century, an unknown scribe collected over two dozen poems into a single volume. The first half dealt with the gods, the later with legendary heroes. Together they encapsulated the heart of the Northern Tradition, specifically as practiced during the Viking Age.

The collection was lost until it resurfaced in the seventeenth century. It was then that Bishop Sveinsson of Skalholt recognized its importance and presented it to the king of Denmark, Frederick III. For the next three centuries, the book was part of the Royal Library in Copenhagen, where it gained the name Codex Regius, "The King's Book," numbered 2365 to differentiate from the others.

In the twentieth century, the Codex Regius was at long last returned to the country of its gestation, Iceland. It was transported under full military escort, and welcomed with fanfare. For Icelanders, it marked the return of their cultural legacy.

The small volume is quarto sized and written in Old Norse. It is for the most part intact, having withstood the ravages of time with little damage. There are some missing pages (probably eight), called the Great Lacuna, but all in all, the book is remarkably well preserved.

The title word, Edda, properly belongs to the treatise of Snorri Sturlusson. Penned in the early thirteenth century, Snorri's *Edda* was intended to teach the skaldic craft to aspiring poets. A large portion of that text is an inspired attempt to collect and codify the myths and legends of the Norsemen. "Edda" is of uncertain origin, and most scholars have attempted to explain it in one of two ways. Either it is derived from the place-name, Oddi, where Snorri studied under Saemund; or it is derived from the Old Norse word for poetry. Both explanations are equally valid, and either way *edda* became a byword for "poetics" following Snorri's work.

When Codex Regius 2365 was first discovered, scholars immediately recognized it as just the sort of collection Snorri must have had access to. Snorri quotes stanzas from many of the poems that can be found in it. For this reason, the material found in Codex Regius 2365 was considered to precede Snorri's work, and it became known as the *Elder Edda*, while Snorri's work became the *Younger Edda*. Another popular custom is to refer to Codex Regius 2365 as the *Poetic Edda*, and Snorri's as the *Prose Edda*.

The text is written in a single hand, although the grammatical styles in the poems indicate the poems came from multiple sources. There are inconsistencies within the work, variations in spelling, and some scribal errors, but taken as a whole, Codex Regius 2365 is an outstanding example of scholarship.

Throughout this work I have utilized the Neckel-Kuhn edition, *Edda; Die Lieder des Codex Regius nebst verwandten Denkmalern.* However, I referenced a facsimile of the original Codex Regius 2365 and deferred to its provenance at all times. The result is a presentation of the Elder Edda with all of its idiosyncrasies intact.

Only a minimal amount of Anglicization was done to the Norse names and special words. For proper names, all accent marks have been dropped. The Icelandic characters "þ" and "ð" have been changed to "th" and "d", "ae" and "œ" have been changed to "ae" and "oe", and all of the various forms of "o" have been rendered as "o". The only exceptions are the special Old Norse terms which are italicized in the text. These words are provided with definitions in the glossary.

As in many ancient manuscripts, Codex Regius 2365 contains a number of large capitals. Generally, these mark the beginnings of poems, but there are exceptions. I have indicated the locations of all the capitals within the text.

Throughout the original are a number of scribal notations. The most significant of these are the marginalia that indicate the speakers within the dialogue poems. I have elected not to include these within this edition because, strictly speaking, they do not belong and interrupt the flow of the poems. The few occurrences that remain are actually given within the main body of the text, not as marginalia. An exception to this is Loki's Gibe, which retains speaker identifications for the convenience of the reader.

I have used titles that are commonly accepted and divided the poems along similar lines, but the reader should be aware that some of these titles and divisions are artificial or based upon information in Norse texts. Notes immediately preceding each section explain such details.

# The Völva's Prophecy

*Untitled*
*Called Völuspá in the Younger Edda*

1 I ask for the hearing of all
the kindred,
greater and lesser
sons of Heimdall;
Valfadir wishes that I
properly tell
the ancient tales of men,
which are earliest remembered.

2 I remember the Jotuns,
born in the early days,
those who long ago
had nurtured me;
I remember nine worlds,
nine wood-dwellers,
the glorious Measure-tree,
underneath the earth.

3 It was the earliest time,
when Ymir lived,
there was no sand nor sea
nor cool waves;
earth was not to be found
nor the upper heaven,
Ginnungar was gaping,
but grass was nowhere.

4 Then Bur's sons
raised it up,
they who Midgard
glorious, shaped;
the sun shone from the south
upon the hall of stone,
then the ground was growing
green leeks.

5 The sun was in the south,
the moon's companion,
her best hand
over heaven's rim;
the sun did not know
where she had a hall,

the stars did not know
where they had homesteads,
the moon did not know
what *megin* he possessed.

6 Then all the Powers went
to Rokstola,
the most holy gods,
and on this gave counsel:
night and the moon-phases,
names were given to them,
morning was named,
and midday,
afternoon and evening,
to count the years.

7 The Aesir met
at Idavoll,
they who altars and temples
had high-timbered,
established forges,
smithed treasures,
shaped tongs
and made tools.

8 Played *tafl* in the courtyard,
they were cheerful,
they had no
want for gold,
until three came,
*thurs* daughters,
very powerful,
from Jotunheimar.

9 Then all the Powers went
to Rokstola,
the most holy gods,
and on this gave counsel:
how should the dwarven
lords be shaped
out of Brimir's blood
and from Blain's limbs.

10 There was Motsognir
who was greatest
of all dwarves,
and Durin another
they were formed like men,
many were made,
dwarves, out of the earth,
as Durin said.

11 Nyi and Nidi,
Nordri and Sudri,
Austri and Vestri,
Althiof, Dvalin,
Bivor, Bavor,
Bombur, Nori,
An and Anar,
Ai, Miodvitnir;

12 Veig and Gandalf,
Vindalf, Thrain,
Thekk and Thorin,
Thror, Vit and Lit,
Nar and Nyrad—
the dwarves I have now
—Regin and Radsvid—
rightly tallied.

13 Fili, Kili,
Fundin, Nali,
Hepti, Vili,
Hanar, Sviur,
Frar, Hornbori,
Fraeg and Loni,
Aurvang, Iari,
Eikinskialdi.

14 Now are told, the dwarves
in Dvalin's company
the kinsmen
tallied with Lofar,
those who went
from the halls of stone
to homes in muddy fields
at Jorovellir.

15 There was Draupnir
and Dolgthrasir,
Har, Haugspori,
Hlevang, Gloi,
Skirvir, Virfir,
Skafid, Ai,
Alf and Yngvi,
Eikinskialdi,
Fialar and Frostri,
Finn and Ginnar;

they will be remembered,
while men live,
the long list of descendants,
that Lofar had.

16 Until three came
from that company,
strong and loving,
Aesir, to the homestead;
found on the land,
capable of little,
Ask and Embla,
ørlög-less;
souls they did not have,
thoughts they did not have,
with no vitality
nor healthy look;

17 Odin gave them souls,
Hoenir gave thoughts,
Lodur gave vitality
and healthy look.

18 I know an ash that stands,
named Yggdrasil,
the highest of trees, dripping
white mud;
thence comes the dew,
that falls in the valley,
the evergreen stands over
Urd's well.

19 Then came the women,
very learned,
three, from the waters,
that are under the tree;
Urd is one named,
another Verdandi
—carved wood-slips—
Skuld is the third.

20 They lay fate,
they determine lives
for the children of men,
declare ørlög.

21 She remembers the troop-slaying,
first in the world,
when Gullveig
was supported by spears
and in Har's hall
she was burned.

22 Thrice burned,
thrice born,

often, not seldom,
though she still lives.

23 Heid they called her,
when she came to their homes,
the fate-revealing *völva*,
she knew spirits;
*seidr* she could do,
*seidr* she knew well,
she was a delight
to evil women.

24 Then all the Powers went
to Rokstola,
the most holy gods,
and on this gave counsel:
whether the Aesir should
pay tribute
or should all the gods
have the offerings.

25 Odin threw out
and shot into the troops,
that was the troop-slaying,
first in the world;
broken was the shield-wall
fortress of the Aesir,
the Vanir used a battle-spell
to tread the valley.

26 Then all the Powers went
to Rokstola,
the most holy gods
and on this gave counsel:
who had in the air
stirred mischief
and to the Jotun race
gave Od's girl.

27 Thor alone did battle,
full of anger,
he seldom sits
when he hears such things;
that oaths were tread upon,
words and promises,
all the binding words,
that between them had passed.

28 She knows Heimdall's
hearing is hidden
under the light-accustomed
holy tree;
and she sees pouring down
a muddy waterfall
from the pledge of Valfadir—

do you know more, and what?

29 Alone she sat outside,
when the old one came
Yggiung of the Aesir,
and looked in her eyes:
"Why do you question me,
why do you put me to the test?
I know all, Odin,
where your eye fell:
it is within the famous
Mimir's well."
Mimir drinks mead
every morning
from the pledge of Valfadir—
do you know more, and what?

30 Herfadir chose for her
arm-rings and necklaces,
gave wise spells
and prophecy-wands;
she could see further and further
into every world.

31 She saw valkyries,
coming from afar,
ready to ride
to Godthiod;
Skuld held a shield,
and Skogul another,
Gunn, Hild, Gondul
and Geirskogul;
now are tallied
Herian's women,
ready to ride
the earth, valkyries.

32 I saw Balder,
the bloody god,
Odin's child,
*ørlög* concealed;
stands there growing,
high in the vale,
slender and very fair,
the mistletoe.

33 It was from that tree,
that seemed glorious,
a dangerous harm-missile,
Hod prepared to shoot;
Balder's brother was
born very quickly,
Odin's son was ready
one night old to slay.

3

34 He never washed his hands
nor combed his head,
until to the pyre he bore
Balder's enemy;
and Frigg wept of grief
in Fensalir
for Valholl's misfortune—
do you know more, and what?

35 She saw laying in bonds
under the ground,
malevolent like
Loki in appearance;
there sat Sigyn
about her companion not at all
she was happy—
do you know more, and what?

36 There falls from the east
out of Eitrdal,
saxes and swords,
Slid it is called.
Standing before the north
at Nidavellir,
a hall of gold
Sindri's lineage;
and another stood
at Okolnir,
the Jotun's drinking hall,
the one named Brimir.

37 She saw a hall standing
far from the sun,
at Nastrond,
the door facing north;
drops of poison fell
in through the smoke-hole,
the hall is braided
of serpents' backs.

38 She saw wading there
in the strong current,
men who perjured
and murder-wolves,
and those who seduced another's
confidant;
there Nidhogg sucks
corpses of those who pass on,
shredding the wolfish ones—
do you know more, and what?

39 In the east sat an old woman
in Jarnvid,
and there gave birth to
the kindred of Fenrir;

out of all of them
a certain one
will devour the moon
in a troll's likeness.

40 Flesh falls
from doomed men,
the seats of the Powers are reddened
with red blood;
black is the sunshine
the summer after,
all weather is hostile—
do you know more, and what?

41 Sitting there on a burial mound
and plucking a harp
the herdsman of *gýgr*,
glad Eggther;
crowing above him
in the bird wood
the fair-red rooster,
who is called Fialar.

42 Crowing over the Aesir
is Gullinkambi,
to wake up the men
in the hall of Heriafadir;
and another is loud
under the earth,
a dirty red rooster,
in the halls of Hel.

43 Garm bays loudly
before Gnipahellir,
the fetters will break,
and the ravenous one runs;
she knows many things,
I see from far away
all the way to Ragnarok,
the mighty gods of battle.

44 Brothers will fight
and until each is dead,
the children of sisters will
spoil their bonds of trust;
it is hard in the world,
much adultery;
battle-age, sword-age,
shields are split,
wind-age, wolf-age,
before the world falls;
man will not
spare another's life.

45 Mim's sons play,

4

and the Measurer burns
near the loud
Giallarhorn;
loudly blows Heimdall,
the horn is taken up,
Odin speaks
with Mim's head;
the old tree groans,
the Jotun is free;
Yggdrasil shakes,
the towering tree.

46 Now Garm bays loudly
before Gnipahellir,
the fetters will break,
and the ravenous one runs;
she knows many things,
I see from far away,
all the way to Ragnarok,
the mighty gods of battle.

47 Hrym comes from the east,
holding a shield before him,
Jormungand writhes
with Jotun-rage,
the serpent is splashing,
and the eagle is screaming,
cutting corpses with a pale beak,
Naglfar is free.

48 A keel comes from the east,
coming close are Muspel's
people upon the waters,
and Loki steers;
the monstrous sons are coming,
all with the ravenous one,
they are with the brother of
Byleist on the voyage.

49 How is it with the Aesir,
how is it with the elves?
All of Jotunheimar roars,
the Aesir are at the Thing;
dwarves groan
before doors of stone,
the kings of the stone walls—
do you know more, and what?

50 Surt journeys from the south
with the wood's enemy,
shining on his sword is
the sun of the gods-of-the-slain;
the rocky cliff crashes down,
greedy women stumble,
men tread the Hel-way,

and the heavens are burst asunder.

51 Then came to Hlin
yet another sorrow,
when Odin goes
to do battle with the wolf,
and Beli's bane,
bright, to Surt;
then will Frigg's
delight fall.

52 Then came the great
son of Sigfadir,
Vidar, striking
at the slaughter-beast;
he came to Hvedrung's son,
caused to stand
a sword in the heart,
then his father was avenged.

53 Then came the glorious
son of Hlodyn,
Odin's son went
to do battle with the wolf;
he dropped in anger
Midgard's guardian,
all men will
have to abandon their homesteads;
nine steps went
Fiorgyn's boy
exhausted from the adder,
with no fear of shame.

54 The sun turns black,
earth sinks into the mist,
no longer crossing the heavens
are the bright shining stars;
raging steam
throughout the life-nourisher,
tall flames play
against heaven itself.

55 Now Garm bays loudly
before Gnipahellir,
the fetters will break,
and the ravenous one runs;
she knows many things,
I see from far away,
all the way to Ragnarok,
the great battle, the fighting gods,

56 She sees coming up
another time
earth from the sea,
growing green;

the waterfall flows,
the eagle flies over
that mountain
hunting for fish.

57 The Aesir meet
at Idavoll
and over the earth-encircling-rope,
mighty, they discuss
Fimbultyr's
ancient runes.

58 There will they later
the wondrous
golden *tafl*-pieces
find in the grass,
those that they in days of old
had owned.

59 Unsown will
the fields grow,
all misfortune will be set right,
Balder will come;
Hod and Balder live together
at Hropt's site of victory,
the gods-of-the-slain are well—

do you know more, and what?

60 Then may Hoenir
choose lot-twigs,
and dwell the sons
of two brothers
in wide Vindheim—
do you know more, and what?

61 She sees a hall standing,
fairer than the sun,
thatched in gold,
at Gimle;
there shall trustworthy
people dwell
and will through all ages
enjoy bliss.

62 There comes the dark
dragon flying,
the glittering adder, beneath,
from Nidafiol;
clearly seen on the wings
—flying over the field—
of Nidhogg, are dead bodies—
now she must sink.

# Háva's Words

*Hávamál*

1 At every doorway,
before going further,
you should look around,
you should look about,
because you cannot know
where enemies
sit on the benches before you.

2 Hail to the host!
A guest has come in,
where shall he sit?
Very quickly
he should go to the hearth,
the one who will be tested.

3 Fire is needed
for whoever comes in
and in the knees is cold;
meat and weeds
the man needs,
whoever journeys over mountains.

4 Water is needed
for whoever to the meal has come,
a dry towel and friendly invitation;
a good disposition,
a treasure if he gets it,
words and silence in return.

5 Wit is needed
for whoever wanders widely,
it is easy to be at home;
he will be subject to derision,
he who knows nothing
and sits among the wise.

6 About his wisdom
no man should be boastful,
his mind should be guarded instead;
then when wise and discreet
he comes to a homestead,
he will seldom be unfortunate;
because a more reliable friend

a man cannot have
than much common sense.

7 The wary guest
who comes to a meal
strains in silent attention;
ears listening
and eyes looking about;
in this way the wise man learns.

8 He is fortunate,
whoever gets
praise and helpful-staves;
that is difficult to get,
when a man shall have
what is in another's breast.

9 He is fortunate,
whoever gets for himself
praise and wisdom during his life;
because bad counsel
men have often received
from another's breast.

10 The best burden
for a man to carry on the road
is much common sense;
better than riches
it will seem in an unknown place,
they are a poor refuge.

11 The best burden
for a man to carry on the road
is much common sense;
worse provisions
when he is across the field
is drinking too much ale;

12 it is not as good,
as good as it is said,
ale for the sons of man;
because there is less wit,
when there are more drinks,
in a man's mind.

13 Ominnis, the heron was called,
who hovered over the ale-drinking,
he steals men's minds;
with this fowl's feathers
I was fettered
in Gunnlod's courtyard.

14 Drunk I was,
excessively drunk
at the wise Fialar's;
that is the best drinking,
when afterwards is retrieved
what was in a man's mind.

15 Silent and thoughtful
should the ruler's son be
and battle-bold;
happy and cheerful
should every man be,
until he meets his bane.

16 The cowardly man
thinks he will always live
if he avoids battle;
but age gives
him no peace,
though spears gave it to him.

17 The fool gapes
when coming to visit,
he mumbles and says nothing;
it will all end at once
if he gets a swallow,
the man's mind is then revealed.

18 That one knows,
who wanders widely
and has journeyed much,
what minds
men have rule over,
who has command of their wits.

19 Men shouldn't hold their cups,
but should drink in moderation,
speak when necessary or not at all;
ill mannered for this
no one will think of you,
if you go to bed early.

20 The gluttonous man,
unless he knows his disposition,
eats in lifelong misery;
often gets ridiculed,
when he comes among the wise,
the foolish man's stomach.

21 The herd knows this,
when they should go home,
and then they leave the field;
but the foolish man
never knows
the measure of his stomach.

22 The man is wretched
and of poor character
who laughs at everyone;
he doesn't know
what he needs to know,
that he is not lacking in flaws.

23 The foolish man
is awake all night
and thinks about everything;
then is weary
when morning comes,
all his troubles are the same.

24 The foolish man
thinks that everyone
smiling at him is his friend;
he doesn't notice,
though they give him animosity,
when he sits with the wise.

25 The foolish man
thinks that everyone
smiling at him is his friend;
then finds that,
when coming to the Thing,
he cannot get an advocate.

26 The foolish man
thinks he knows all,
if he stays in the corner;
he doesn't know this
what he should say
if he is put to the test by others.

27 The fool
who comes among the people,
it is best, that he stays quiet;
no one will know
that he has no knowledge,
except that he talks too much;
the men know
that he knows nothing,
when he talks too much.

28 Wise he seems to be,
if he knows how to question
and answer as well;

nothing is concealed
by the sons of men,
what is going around the people.

29 Crazy speech,
by he who is never silent,
senseless staves;
the tongue quick to speak,
unless if it is held,
often calls down evil.

30 An object of scorn
a man shouldn't make of another,
when he comes to visit;
many seem to be wise,
if they are not put to the test,
and remain unmolested if silent.

31 He thinks himself wise,
whoever takes flight
when guests mock guests;
he doesn't know,
whoever was sneering,
if he is making noise with enemies.

32 Many people
are kind to each other,
but at feasts will quarrel;
strife among men
there will always be,
guests quarreling with guests.

33 An early meal
men should often get,
unless they are coming to visit;
sitting and snooping,
the manner of the famished,
and without any debate.

34 It is a great detour
to go to a bad friend,
even though he lives on the way;
but to a good friend
the way lies straight,
even though he is farther away.

35 You should go,
should not be a guest
always in one place;
love is not given
if you sit too long
at another's bench-place.

36 A farm is better,
even though it is little,

everyone is a man at home;
though he doesn't have two goats
and has ropes for rafters,
it is better than begging.

37 A farm is better,
even though it is little,
everyone is a man at home;
bleeding are the hearts,
of they who must ask
at every meal for meat.

38 His weapons
a man on the field should not
walk away from one step;
because one cannot know
if when stepping outside
a spear will be needed.

39 I never met a generous man
or one liberal with food
that would not accept a gift,
or one who's property
was not . . .,
to refuse a reward, if offered.

40 His property,
what he has amassed,
a man should not need to suffer for;
often what is saved,
what is intended for loved ones,
goes much worse than is intended.

41 Weapons and weeds
shall gladden friends,
that should be self-evident;
people who exchange gifts often
are friends the longest,
if it turns out well.

42 To his friend
a man should be a friend
and repay gift with gift;
laughter with laughter
should the sons of men take,
and falsehood with lies.

43 To his friends
a man should be a friend,
to them and their friends;
but to his enemies
should no man
be a friend.

44 You know, if you have a friend,

9

one that you trust well,
and you would get good from him:
share your thoughts with him
and exchange gifts,
go to visit him often.

45 If you have another,
that you don't trust well,
but you would get good from him:
you should speak beautifully
but think deceitfully
and repay falsehood with lies.

46 Furthermore for him,
the one that you poorly trust
and are suspicious of his mind:
you should laugh with him
but speak not of your spirit,
repaying gifts equally.

47 I was young long ago,
I traveled alone,
then I went astray;
but thought myself rich,
when I found another,
man is the joy of man.

48 Generous, brave
men love the best,
seldom nursing anxiety;
but the cowardly man
fears everything,
the miser cringes at gifts.

49 My weeds
I gave on the road
to two wooden-men;
they were considered as kings,
when they had clothes,
the naked man is despised.

50 The tree withers
on the bare hillock,
it is unprotected by bark or needles;
and so the man
that no one loves,
why should he live long?

51 Hotter than fire
burning between bad friends
peace for five days;
but then it is slaked
when the sixth comes,
and the friendship deteriorates.

52 Not much
should a man give,
often a bargain is a little praise;
with a half a loaf
and with a tilted cup
I took a fellow to me.

53 Little sands,
little seas
little are men's minds;
thus all men
are not evenly wise,
all men are imperfect.

54 Middle-wise
every man should be,
never too wise;
those men
have fair lives,
who don't know too much.

55 Middle-wise
every man should be,
never too wise;
because the wise man's heart
is seldom glad,
if he is too wise.

56 Middle-wise
every man should be,
never too wise;
his *ørlög*
no one can know beforehand,
and still have a mind free of anxiety.

57 Brand gets from brand
blaze, until it is also burning,
a fire quickens by fire;
man gets from man
knowledge by talking,
but gets foolishness from silence.

58 He should rise early,
who would of another
take wealth and life;
seldom does the sleeping wolf
get the leg,
nor is the sleeping man victorious.

59 He should rise early,
who has few workers,
and go to see to his work;
he is much delayed,
who in the morning stays in bed,
wealth is half won by the energetic.

60 Dry boards
and birchbark thatch,
these can man measure correctly,
and of the wood,
he may need for
a quarter-year or season.

61 Washed and full
a man should ride to the Thing,
even though his weeds are poor;
by shoes and breeches
a man is not shamed,
nor by his horse,
even if he doesn't have good ones.

62 Questions and answers
every learned man shall have
who would be called wise;
one knows
but another should not,
everyone knows, if three.

63 Snapping and stretching his neck
when he comes to the sea,
the eagle over old waters;
in this way the man
who comes among many men
and looks for an advocate.

64 His power
should every wise ruler
have in moderation;
he will find,
when he comes among the bold,
that no one is the keenest.

65 Those words,
that one man says to another,
often he gets paid back.

66 Very early in the day
I have come to many homesteads,
and too late to some;
the ale was drunk,
some was not brewed,
the uninvited rarely gets a drink.

67 Here and everywhere
I have been invited to a home,
I did not need meat to eat,
or two legs
hung at a true friend's,
when I had eaten one.

68 Fire is best

for the sons of men
and the sight of the sun,
his health,
if a man can have it,
a life without defect.

69 No man is completely unfortunate,
though he has bad luck;
some are blessed with sons,
some with kinsmen,
some with ample possessions,
some with good work.

70 Better to be living
and happily alive,
the living gets the cow;
I saw the fires burning high
for the rich man,
but he lay dead outside the door.

71 The lame ride horses,
the one-armed drive herds,
the deaf fight and dig in;
better to be blind,
rather than burned:
dead men are useless to everyone.

72 A son is better
though he is born late
after the man is dead;
seldom do memorial stones
stand beside the road
unless raised by kin for kin.

73 Two can harry one,
the tongue is the head's bane,
it seems to me in every fur coat
a hand is expected;
74 the evening meal is pleasing
to one who trusts his provisions,
short are a ship's berths,
shifting are autumn nights;
many kinds of weather
in five days,
even more in a month.

75 He knows,
who knows nothing,
that many men are fools with money;
one is rich,
another is not rich,
he should not be blamed for that.

76 Cattle die,
kinsmen die,

11

you yourself will die as well;
but words of honor
never die,
for whoever gets good ones.

77 Cattle die,
kinsmen die,
you yourself will die as well;
I know one thing,
it never dies:
the reputation of the dead.

78 Full sheepfolds
I saw before Fitiung's sons,
now they carry beggar's staves;
this is how wealth goes
in the blink of an eye,
it is the most unreliable of friends.

79 The foolish man,
if he gets possession
of wealth or a woman's love,
his pride grows,
but not his common sense,
he goes deeper into his delusion.

80 When it is known,
what you asked the runes,
the ones from the Powers,
those from the highest Power
and colored by the mighty sage,
it would be best if you stayed silent.

81 Praise the day in the evening,
a woman, when burned,
a sword, when tested,
a maiden, when given,
ice, when over it,
ale, when drank.

82 In wind you should chop wood,
in good weather row on the sea,
in the darkness talk with a girl:
the day has many eyes;
a ship should be used to glide,
and a shield to protect,
a sword to cut,
and a maid to kiss.

83 Drink ale by the fire,
and slide over ice,
acquire a meager horse,
and a dirty sword,
fatten the horse at home,
and a hound at the farm.

84 A maiden's words
shall no man trust,
nor what is said by a woman;
because on a spinning wheel
their hearts were shaped,
they have the ability to change.

85 A broken bow,
a blazing fire,
a yawning wolf,
a cawing crow,
a grunting swine,
a rootless tree,
a growing wave,
a boiling kettle;

86 a flying arrow,
a falling wave,
ice one-night old,
a serpent lying coiled,
a bride's bed talk
or a broken sword,
a bear's play
or a king's child;

87 a sick calf,
a self-willed thrall,
a pleasant-speaking *völva*,
a corpse newly fallen,

88 an acre early sown
no man should trust,
nor too early in a son;
weather rules the acre,
and brains the son,
risky are they both.

89 Your brother's killer,
if you meet on the road,
a house half-burned,
a horse too swift—
the horse is useless,
if it breaks a leg—
no man should be so trusting,
that he trusts all of these.

90 So is the loose tongue of a woman,
they have deceitful words,
like driving horses without ice-spikes
on slippery ice,
frolicsome, two-winters-old,
poorly broke,
or using in a strong wind
a rudderless boat,
or the lame trying to catch
reindeer on the mountain.

91 Plainly now I speak,
because I have known both:
fickle are men's spirits with women;
we speak most beautifully
when we speak to deceive,
that tricks the wisest mind.

92 He should speak beautifully
and offer valuable gifts,
whoever would have a woman's love,
praise the body
of the shining girl;
he gets, who flatters.

93 Reproach for love
should no man
of another do;
often the wise man is taken,
but the fool is not taken,
by ravishing looks.

94 Not reproach one bit
should a man of another do,
for what befalls many men;
fools out of the wise
the sons of men are made
by mighty desire.

95 The spirit alone knows
what dwells in the heart,
he alone knows his feelings;
no sickness is worse
for wise men
than to have nobody to love.

96 That I learned when
I sat in the reeds
and waited for my desire;
body and heart
the wise girl was to me,
yet I did not get to hold her.

97 Billing's maiden
I found on the bed,
bright as the sun, asleep;
nobleman's pleasures
I thought were nothing,
except to live with that body.

98 "Again before evening
should you, Odin, come,
if you will speak with the woman;
all will be in chaos,
if anyone knows
such a shameful deed together."

99 I turned away,
and thought to love,
from my desire;
this I thought,
that I would have
all her desire and play.

100 So I came next time,
there were efficient
warriors awake all around;
with bright fires
and carrying torches,
so the miserable way was marked.

101 And near morning,
when I again came around,
when the household was asleep;
a bitch I then found
of the good woman
tied to the bed.

102 Many a good maid,
if you get acquainted with her,
is fickle with men;
I found that out,
when the wise-in-counsel
woman I tried to seduce to shame;
every kind of humiliation
the wise woman laid out for me,
and I did not have her for a wife.

103 At home a man is happy
and cheerful with his guest,
astute he should be about himself,
mindful and eloquent,
if he would be very knowledgeable,
he should speak of good things;
the greatest of fools
he is called, whoever can't say much,
that is the fool's nature.

104 The old Jotun I visited,
now I have come again,
silence got me nothing there;
many words
I spoke to my advantage
in Suttung's hall.

105 Gunnlod gave me
a golden stool and
a drink of the precious mead;
a poor payment in return
I let her have afterwards
for her sincere spirit,
for her sorrowful feelings,

13

for her weary mind.

106 With a gimlet's mouth
I made room for myself
and gnawed through the rock;
over and under me
stood the path of Jotuns,
and so I risked my head.

107 The easily bargained
I have made good use of,
few are the wise man's wants;
because Odrerir
has now come up
to the world's ancient temples.

108 It is clear to me
that I would not have come
out of the Jotun's courtyard,
if I did not use Gunnlod,
the good woman,
the one I laid my arms around.

109 The next day
the rime-*thursar* came
to ask Havi for advice
in Havi's hall;
they asked about Bolverk,
if he had come in bonds
or if he had visited Suttung.

110 Odin's ring-oath
I thought he had swore,
how can we trust his loyalty?
Suttung was deceived
when he let him drink
and Gunnlod weeps.

111 It is time to recite
from the wise one's stool,
at Urd's well;
I saw and kept silent,
I saw and considered,
I listened to the speech of men;
of runes I heard discussion,
nor did they keep silent their advice,
at Havi's hall,
in Havi's hall;
I heard them say:

112 I counsel you, Loddfafnir,
to take this advice,
you will profit, if you take it,
it will do you good, if you get it:

at night you should not rise,
except to look about
or if you need to relieve yourself.

113 I counsel you, Loddfafnir,
to take this advice,
you will profit, if you take it,
it will do you good, if you get it:
a woman skilled in magic
you should not take to your bed,
so that she holds your limbs;

114 she will make it,
so you do not care about
the Thing or the king's speech;
you won't want meat
or anyone's fellowship,
you will go to bed in sorrow.

115 I counsel you, Loddfafnir,
to take this advice,
you will profit, if you take it,
it will do you good, if you get it:
another's wife
you should never seduce
to be a confidante.

116 I counsel you, Loddfafnir,
to take this advice,
you will profit, if you take it,
it will do you good, if you get it:
on a mountain or fjord
if you desire to go,
you should be well fed.

117 I counsel you, Loddfafnir,
to take this advice,
you will profit, if you take it,
it will do you good, if you get it:
an evil man
you should never let
misfortunes of yours know;
because of an evil man
you will never get
in payment a good spirit.

118 A high-placed wound
I saw on a man
because of an evil woman's words;
a deceitful tongue
was death to him,
and he was unjustly accused.

119 I counsel you, Loddfafnir,
to take this advice,
you will profit, if you take it,

it will do you good, if you get it:
you know, if you have a friend,
that you trust well,
you should go visit often;
because brushwood grows
and high grass
on the way, if no one treads it.

120 I counsel you, Loddfafnir,
to take this advice,
you will profit, if you take it,
it will do you good, if you get it:
a good man
attract to yourself with joy-runes
and always get helpful *galdr*.

121 I counsel you, Loddfafnir,
to take this advice,
you will profit, if you take it,
it will do you good, if you get it:
with your friend
should you never
be first to break bonds;
sorrow eats the heart
if you are unable to tell
someone all your feelings.

122 I counsel you, Loddfafnir,
to take this advice,
you will profit, if you take it,
it will do you good, if you get it:
word exchange
you should never have
with a foolish ape;
123 because from the evil man
you will never
get good in return;
but a good man
will get for you
many assurances of praise.

124 They have a bond of kinship,
whoever can tell you
all their thoughts;
everything is better
than to be fickle;
he is a poor friend
if he will not tell.

125 I counsel you, Loddfafnir,
to take this advice,
you will profit, if you take it,
it will do you good, if you get it:
three words of quarrel
never have with a worse man;

often the better is beaten
when the worse one fights.

126 I counsel you, Loddfafnir,
to take this advice,
you will profit, if you take it,
it will do you good, if you get it:
you shouldn't be a shoemaker,
nor a fletcher,
except for yourself alone;
if the shoe is poorly shaped,
or the shaft is bent,
misfortune will be called upon you.

127 I counsel you, Loddfafnir,
to take this advice,
you will profit, if you take it,
it will do you good, if you get it:
wherever you recognize trouble,
you should curse at it,
and don't give the fiend peace.

128 I counsel you, Loddfafnir,
to take this advice,
you will profit, if you take it,
it will do you good, if you get it:
pleased by evil
you should never be,
but let yourself be by good.

129 I counsel you, Loddfafnir,
to take this advice,
you will profit, if you take it,
it will do you good, if you get it:
look up
you should not do in battle—
like madmen
the sons of men who do—
lest you be bewitched.

130 I counsel you, Loddfafnir,
to take this advice,
you will profit, if you take it,
it will do you good, if you get it:
if you want have a good woman
to speak joy-runes to
and get pleasure from,
you should make beautiful promises
and hold to them tightly,
no man loathes good, if he gets it.

131 I counsel you, Loddfafnir,
to take this advice,
you will profit, if you take it,
it will do you good, if you get it:

I want you to be wary,
but not over-wary;
be most wary with ale
and with another's wife,
and with this third,
that thieves don't make sport of you.

132 I counsel you, Loddfafnir,
to take this advice,
you will profit, if you take it,
it will do you good, if you get it:
to scorn nor derision
you should never subject
a guest or wanderer!

133 Often you do not really know,
about those sitting before you,
whose kin has come in,
no man is so good,
as to be without blemish
nor so bad as to be worthless.

134 I counsel you, Loddfafnir,
to take this advice,
you will profit, if you take it,
it will do you good, if you get it:
at the high sage
you should never laugh!
Often is good,
what the old say;
often from a shriveled mouth
discerning words come,
those who hang with the hides
and swing with the skins
and waver with the wretches.

135 I counsel you, Loddfafnir,
to take this advice,
you will profit, if you take it,
it will do you good, if you get it:
you should not bark at guests
or abuse them with the locked door,
you should treat the poor well!

136 That is a strong bar
that must swing
to open for everyone;
give an arm-ring,
or they will call down curses
on your every limb.

137 I counsel you, Loddfafnir,
to take this advice,
you will profit, if you take it,
it will do you good, if you get it:

wherever you drink ale
you should call upon earth's *megin*
because the earth absorbs ale,
and fire with sickness,
oak with constipation,
an ear of grain with magic,
the hall with domestic quarrels—
for hatred invoke the moon—
earthworm with insect bites,
and runes with evil;
use the ground with floods.

138 **I** know, that I hung
on the windswept tree
all of nine nights,
spear wounded
and given to Odin,
myself to myself,
on that tree,
that no man knows,
where its roots run.

139 I wasn't favored with loaves
or with the horn,
I looked underneath me;
I took up the runes,
took them screaming,
then I fell back down.

140 Nine powerful songs
I took from the renowned son of
Bolthor, Bestla's father,
and I got a drink
of the precious mead,
poured from Odrerir.

141 Then I took seed
and became learned
and grew and thrived;
my words were
becoming other words,
my deeds
were leading to other deeds.

142 Runes you must find
and legible staves,
very mighty staves,
very powerful staves,
that the mighty sage colored
and the mighty Powers made
and the invoker of power *ríst*.

143 Odin among the Aesir,
and Dain for the elves,

16

Dvalin for the dwarves,
Asvid for the Jotuns,
I *ríst* some for myself.

144 Do you know how to *ríst*,
do you know how to read?
Do you know how to color,
do you know how to test?
Do you know how to pray,
do you know how to sacrifice?
Do you know how to offer,
do you know how to slaughter?

145 Better not to pray
than to sacrifice too much,
a gift demands compensation;
better not to offer gifts
than to offer too much.
So Thund *ríst*
before mankind existed;
where he rose up,
when he came down.

146 I know those songs,
that a ruler's wife doesn't know
nor anyone's son;
"help," one is called,
and it will help you
with quarrels and troubles
and all affection.

147 I know another one
that the sons of man need
those who will live as healers.

148 I know a third one,
if it seems very necessary to me
to fetter men that hate me:
edges it dulls
of my adversaries,
their weapons and clubs won't bite.

149 I know a fourth one,
if people put me
in bonds on my limbs:
I can sing
so I may go,
fetters spring from my feet
and shackles from my hands.

150 I know a fifth one,
if I see in flight
a missile shot into the troops:
it cannot fly so forcefully
that I cannot stop it,
if I see it with my eyes.

151 I know a sixth one,
if a man wounds me
with the sappy roots of a tree:
and the man,
who provoked my wrath,
the harm consumes him, not me.

152 I know a seventh one,
if I see high flames
in the hall around my bench-mates:
it doesn't burn so widely
that I cannot rescue them,
I know the *galdr* to intone.

153 I know an eighth one,
which is to everyone
very useful to know:
wherever hate grows
between the sons of warriors,
there I may quickly make amends.

154 I know a ninth one,
if I stand in need,
to save a traveler at sea:
I calm the wind
on the waves
and calm all the sea.

155 I know a tenth one,
if I see a fence-rider
playing in the sky:
I can make it so
they go astray from
their real form,
their real spirit.

156 I know an eleventh one,
if I should to battle
lead old friends:
under shield I chant
and they go triumphantly
unharmed to battle,
unharmed from battle,
they go everywhere without harm.

157 I know a twelfth one,
if I see up in a tree
a wavering hanged-corpse:
I can *ríst*
and color runes
so that the man moves
and talks with me.

158 I know a thirteenth one,
if I should a young boy

17

throw water on:
he will not fall
though he goes into battle,
the man will not sink before swords.

159 I know a fourteenth one,
if I should before the troops
recount the gods:
Aesir and elves
I know about them all,
few of the foolish know this.

160 I know a fifteenth one,
which Thiodrorir chanted,
the dwarf, before Delling's doors:
he chanted strongly to the Aesir,
and before the elves,
Hroptatyr's wisdom.

161 I know a sixteenth one,
if I desire from a wise woman
to have all desire and pleasure:
I turn the spirit
of the white-armed woman
and I completely change her mind.

162 I know a seventeenth one,
that I will never be shunned by
the maiden girls.
These songs
you will, Loddfafnir,
want for a long time;
but they're good if you get them,
useful, if you learn them,
needful, if you accept them.

163 I know an eighteenth one,
that I never teach
to maids nor another's wife—
it is better,
if only one knows
what belongs at the end of songs—
except one
who was in my arms
or is my sister.

164 Now Havi's Words have been recited,
in Havi's hall,
very needful for the sons of men,
useless for the sons of Jotuns;
Hail, to the one who says it,
hail, to the one who learns it!
Beneficial, for one who learns,
holy, for they who listen.

# Vafdrudner's Tale

## Vafþrúðnismal

1 Counsel me now, Frigg,
because I desire to go
to visit Vafdrudnir;
very curious
I will speak about ancient words
with the all-wise Jotun.

2 Keep at home
I would Heriafadir
in the enclosure of the gods,
because no Jotun
I know is equally mighty
as Vafdrudnir is.

3 Much I have traveled,
much I have challenged,
much I have tested the Powers,
I want to know this,
what Vafdrudnir
has in his home.

4 Safe as you go,
safe as you come back,
safe as you travel!
Your intellect is worthy,
you should go, Aldafadir,
match words with the Jotun.

5 Odin left then
to test with words
the all-wise Jotun;
he came to the hall
owned by Im's father,
Ygg went inside.

6 Hail to you, Vafdrudnir!
I have now come to your hall,
to see you yourself;
this will I know first:
if you are knowledgeable
and all-wise, Jotun.

7 Who is this man,

in my house
throwing words at me?
You will not come
out of our hall,
unless you prove yourself wisest.

8 Gagnrad I am called;
now I am going to come
thirsty into your hall;
needing hospitality,
I have traveled far,
and your welcome, Jotun.

9 Why do you, Gagnrad,
speak this way from the floor?
Sit on the benches in my hall
then we shall put to the test
who has more wisdom,
the guest or the old sage.

10 A not-rich man,
when coming to the rich,
speaks when necessary and quickly;
too many words
I am certain will get ill,
whoever has come with cold ribs.

11 You tell me, Gagnrad,
since you will stay on the floor
pressing onward with your test,
what is that horse called,
that which draws
day to mankind.

12 Skinfaxi is his name,
he that draws the shining
day to mankind;
the best of all horses
he seems among the Hreidgotar,
the horse's mane always shines.

13 You tell me this, Gagnrad,
since you will stay on the floor

pressing onward with your test,
what is that steed called,
that from the east draws
night to the helpful Powers.

14 Hrimfaxi is his name,
he which draws
night to the helpful Powers;
bit-foam
falls from him in the morning,
thence comes dew in the valley.

15 You tell me this, Gagnrad,
since you will stay on the floor
pressing onward with your test,
what is that called
which divides the Jotuns sons'
ground from the gods.

16 Ifing it is called,
which divides the Jotun sons'
ground from the gods;
open it runs
and shall do so for all days,
no ice forms on the river.

17 You tell me this, Gagnrad,
since you will stay on the floor
pressing onward with your test,
what is the field called,
where they assemble for war
Surt and the beloved gods.

18 Vigrid the field is called,
where they assemble for war
Surt and the beloved gods;
a hundred *rastir*
it measures on each side,
that is the appointed field.

19 Now you are wise, guest,
you can come to the Jotun's bench,
and talk on the seats together!
Wager heads
we shall in the hall
guest, on our wisdom.

20 You tell this first,
if your intellect is enough,
and you, Vafdrudnir, know,
where did the earth come from
and the upper heavens
in the beginning, wise Jotun.

21 Out of Ymir's flesh

was the earth shaped,
and out of bones the mountains,
heaven out of the skull
of the rime-cold Jotun,
and out of his blood the sea.

22 You tell this second,
if your intellect is enough,
and you, Vafdrudnir, know,
where did the moon come from,
that journeys over men,
and the sun as well.

23 Mundilfoeri he is called,
he is Mani's father
and Sol the same;
spinning through heaven
they shall be every day,
counting years in the ages.

24 You tell this third,
since they say you are wise
and you, Vafdrudnir, know,
where did the day come from,
that journeys over mankind,
and night with the moon-phases.

25 Delling he is called,
he is Dag's father,
and Nott was born of Nor,
waxing and waning
the helpful Powers shaped,
counting years in the ages.

26 You tell this fourth,
since they say you are learned
and you, Vafdrudnir, know,
where did winter come from
and warm summer
first with the learned Powers.

27 Vindsval he is called,
he is Vetr's father,
and Svasud is Sumar's.

28 You tell this fifth,
since they say you are learned
and you, Vafdrudnir, know,
who was eldest of the Aesir
and Ymir's kinsmen
in days of old.

29 Countless winters ago,
before the earth was shaped,
that was when Bergelmir was born,

Thrudgelmir
was his father,
and Aurgelmir his grandfather.

30 You tell this sixth,
since they say you are wise
and you, Vafdrudnir, know,
whence did Aurgelmir
come with Jotuns sons
first, wise Jotun.

31 From Elivagar
drops of poison flew,
and grew until a Jotun was made.

32 You tell this seventh,
since they say you are wise
and you, Vafdrudnir, know,
how did he get children,
that bold Jotun,
since he had no sport with women.

33 Under his arms grew
they say, rime-*thursar*
men and women together;
foot with foot
begat the learned Jotun
a six-headed son.

34 You tell this eighth,
since they say you are learned
and you, Vafdrudnir, know,
what do you first remember
and earliest know;
you are all-wise Jotun.

35 Countless winters ago,
before the earth was shaped,
that was when Bergelmir was born,
I remember first that
when the learned Jotun
was lying on the mill-stand.

36 You tell this ninth,
since they say you are wise
and you, Vafdrudnir, know,
whence does the wind come
that journeys over the sea;
but men themselves never see it.

37 Hraesvelg he is called,
sitting at heaven's end,
a Jotun in an eagle's likeness,
from his wings,
they say, wind comes

over all men.

38 You tell this tenth,
since you the god's destiny
entirely, Vafdrudnir, know,
how did Niord come
to be with the sons of the Aesir;
temples and stone altars
beyond count he rules,
and he was not born of the Aesir.

39 In Vanaheim
the Powers shaped him
and gave him to the gods as hostage.
at Aldarrok
he will come back
home with wise Vanir.

40 You tell me this eleventh,
where men in the yard
fight each other every day.

41 All the *einheriar*
in Odin's courtyard
fight each other every day;
they choose who will be slain
and ride from the battle,
afterwards they sit reconciled.

42 You tell this twelfth,
why you the god's destiny
entirely, Vafdrudnir, know;
secrets from the Jotuns
and all the gods
you truly tell,
all-wise Jotun.

43 Secrets from the Jotuns
and all the gods
I can consent to tell,
because to every world I have come,
I went to nine worlds
down into Niflhel,
there dead men go from Hel.

44 Many times I traveled,
many times I challenged,
many times I tested Powers:
what men live,
after the end of the famous
Fimbulvetr is with them?

45 Lif and Lifthrasir,
and they will hide
in Hoddmimir's wood;

21

morning-dew
they will have for food,
from them all people come.

46 Many times I traveled,
many times I challenged,
many times I tested Powers:
whence will the sun come
into the flat heavens,
when Fenrir ends this one?

47 A daughter
borne by Alfrodul,
before Fenrir brought her to an end;
she shall ride,
after the Powers die,
the girl on her mother's road.

48 Many times I traveled,
many times I challenged,
many times I tested Powers:
who are those maidens,
gliding over the sea,
traveling with much understanding?

49 Three hosts
fall over the settlements
Mogthrasir's girls,
*hamingia* all
they are in the world
though Jotuns raised them.

50 Many times I traveled,
many times I challenged,
many times I tested Powers:
who'll have authority over the Aesir
and the possessions of the gods,
after Surt's blaze is slaked?

51 Vidar and Vali,
dwell in the sanctuaries of the gods,
after Surt's blaze is slaked;
Modi and Magni
shall have Miollnir
and bring the cessation of battle.

52 Many times I traveled,
many times I challenged,
many times I tested Powers:
what was Odin's
cause of death,
when the Powers are destroyed?

53 The wolf swallowed
Aldafadir,
for this Vidar will wreak vengeance;
cold jaws
he will cleave
of the wolf in battle.

54 Many times I traveled,
many times I challenged,
many times I tested Powers:
what did Odin say
before the pyre was set,
himself into his son's ear?

55 No man knows that,
what you in days of old
said in your son's ear;
the doomed mouth
of mine spoke ancient lore
and of Ragnarok.

56 Now I with Odin
contended with my wise words,
you will always be the wisest.

# Grimnir's Tale

*Grímnismál*

King Hraudung had two sons; one was named Agnar, and the other Geirrod. Agnar was ten winters old, and Geirrod was eight winters. The two rowed a boat, with their fishing line, to catch small fish. The wind drove them out to sea. In the darkness of night they crashed into the shore, and went up and met a cottager. They were there for the winter. An old woman fostered Agnar and the old man Geirrod.

In the spring the old man got them a ship. And when the old woman led them to the shore, then the old man spoke alone with Geirrod. They obtained wind and came to rest at their father's place. Geirrod was forward in the ship, he leapt up onto the land and rushed out of the ship and said: "You go, let the evil one have you!" The ship sailed out. And Geirrod went up to the farmstead. He was well received. Then his father was deceased. Geirrod was then taken to be king and was a splendid man.

Odin and Frigg sat on Hlidskialf and saw into all the worlds. Odin spoke: "You see Agnar, your fosterling, where he is fathering children with a *gýgr* in a cave? But Geirrod, my fosterling, is king and sits now on land." Frigg said: "He is so stingy with food that he abuses his guests if he thinks too many have come." Odin said that this was the greatest lie. They made a wager on the matter.

Frigg sent her handmaiden, Fulla, to Geirrod. She told the king to beware, that a man skilled in magic was trying to bewitch him, he had come into the land, and she said that it would mark him that no dog was so vicious that it would jump on him. And that was the greatest lie, that Geirrod was not generous with food. Although he did have that man seized, he who no dog would attack. That man was in a blue cloak and named Grimnir, and said nothing more about himself, although he was asked. The king had him tortured until he would talk and set him between two fires, and he sat there eight nights. King Geirrod had a son, ten winters old, and named Agnar after his brother. Agnar went to Grimnir and gave him a full horn to drink, saying that the king was treating him badly, to cause an innocent man to be tortured. Grimnir drank from it. Then the fires were coming close to burning the cloak of Grimnir. He said:

1 Hot you are, hastener,
and much too great,
go away, fire!
My loden is singed,
though I lift it high,
my cloak burns before me.

2 Eight nights
I sat here between the fires,
and no one offered a drink to me,
except this one Agnar,

and he will be given authority,
Geirrod's son,
in the land of the Goths.

3 You shall have good luck, Agnar,
because you are blessed
by Veratyr;
one drink
you shall never
get better payment for.

23

4 The land is holy,
that I see laying
near the Aesir and elves,
and in Thrudheim
Thor shall be,
until the Powers are destroyed.

5 Ydalir it is called,
that is where Ull has
his hall established;
Alfheim to Frey
was given in days of old
for tooth-payment by the gods.

6 There is a third settlement,
the blithe Powers
thatched the hall in silver,
Valaskialf it is called,
it was well built by
the Aesir in days of old.

7 Sokkvabekk the fourth is called,
and there may cool
waves crash over;
there Odin and Saga
drink throughout the day
glad, out of golden goblets.

8 Gladsheim the fifth is called,
there is gold-bright
Valholl located;
and there Hropt
chooses every day
those slain by weapons.

9 It is very easily recognized,
by those who come to Odin,
when they see the hall;
spears for the house's rafters,
shields for the house's thatching,
armor strewn on the benches.

10 It is very easily recognized,
by those who come to Odin,
when they see the hall;
a wolf hangs
before the west door,
and an eagle hovers over it.

11 Thrymheim the sixth is called,
it was Thiazi's homestead,
the very powerful Jotun;
but now Skadi dwells,
the god's bright bride,
in her father's ancient home.

12 Breidablik is the seventh,
and there Balder has
his hall established,
in the land,
where I know lay
few baleful runes.

13 Himinbiorg is the eighth
and there Heimdall
is said to rule sanctuaries;
the guardian goes there
to drink in the comfortable house,
glad, in good amounts.

14 Folkvang is the ninth,
and there Freyia rules
choice seats in the hall;
half of the dead
she selects every day,
and half goes to Odin.

15 Glitnir is the tenth,
it is supported by gold
and silver as well;
and there Forseti
dwells most days
and calms all quarrels.

16 Noatun is the eleventh,
and there Niord has
his hall established;
the prince of men,
free of fault,
rules the high-timbered sanctuary.

17 Brushwood grows
and high grass
in Vidar's land, widely,
and there the son declares
from the back of his horse,
boldly, to avenge his father.

18 Andhrimnir
has in Eldhrimnir
Saehrimnir's broth,
the best pork,
but few know this,
with what the *einheriar* are fed.

19 Geri and Freki
accustomed to war are fed by
glorious Heriafadir;
but with wine alone
the weapon-glorious
Odin always lives.

20 Hugin and Munin
fly out every day
over the immense earth;
I fear for Hugin
that he will not come back,
but even more for Munin.

21 Noisy Thund,
vigilant Thiodvitnir's
fish in the flood;
the river's current
seems too great
for the rejoicing dead to wade.

22 Valgrind it is called,
standing in the plain,
mighty, before the holy doors;
the gate is ancient,
but few know this,
how that bar is locked.

23 Five hundred doors
and four tens,
I know Bilskirnir has all around;
of those houses,
that I know are roofed,
I know my son's is greatest.

24 Five hundred doors
and four tens,
I know are in Valholl;
eight hundred *einheriar*
walk through one door,
when they go to attack the wolf.

25 Heidrun the goat is called
standing on Heriafadir's hall
and biting on Laerad's branches;
fill the drinking barrel
he shall with shining mead,
that liquor will not run out.

26 Eikthyrnir the deer is called
standing on Heriafadir's hall
and biting on Laerad's branches;
and from his horns
Hvergelmir drips,
from there all waters come.

27 Sid and Vid,
Soekin and Eikin,
Svol and Gunnthro,
Fiorm and Fimbulthul,
Rhine and Rennandi,
Gipul and Gopul,

Gomul and Geirvimul,
they flow over the god's hoard,
Thyn and Vin,
Thol and Hol,
Grad and Gunnthorin;

28 Vina one is called,
another is Vegsvin,
the third is Thiodnuma,
Nyt and Not,
Non and Hron,
Slid and Hrid,
Sylg and Ylg,
Vid and Van,
Vond and Strond,
Giol and Leipt,
they fall near men,
and fall to Hel afterwards.

29 Kormt and Ormt,
and the two Kerlaug,
there shall Thor wade,
every day,
when he goes to sit in judgment
at the ash Yggdrasil;
because the Aesir bridge
burns all in flames,
the holy waters seethe.

30 Glad and Gyllir,
Glaer and Skeidbrimir,
Silfrintopp and Sinir,
Gisl and Falhofnir,
Gulltopp and Lettfeti,
they are rode by the Aesir,
every day,
when they go to sit in judgment
at the ash Yggdrasil.

31 Three roots
extend in three ways
under the ash Yggdrasil;
Hel lives under one,
another the rime-*thursar*,
the third, mankind.

32 Ratatosk the squirrel is called,
that shall run
upon the ash Yggdrasil,
the eagle's words
he shall carry down
and tell Nidhogg below.

33 And there are four deer,
on the growing buds they
gnaw with bent-necks:

Dain and Dvalin,
Duneyr and Durathror.

34 More serpents
lay under the ash Yggdrasil
than thought of by any stupid ape;
Goin and Moin
—they are Grafvitnir's sons—
Grabak and Grafvollud
Ofnir and Svafnir
I think shall always
gnaw the tree's limbs.

35 The ash Yggdrasil
suffers hardships
more than men think;
deer bite it above,
and the sides decay,
Nidhogg gnaws below.

36 Hrist and Mist
I wish would bring me a horn,
Skeggiold and Skogul,
Hild and Thrud,
Hlok and Herfiotur,
Gol and Geirolul,
Randgrid and Radgrid
and Reginleif,
they bring the *einheriar* ale.

37 Arvak and Alsvid,
they shall up from here,
exhausted, drag the sun;
and under their bows
placed the happy Powers,
the Aesir, iron bellows.

38 Svol it is called,
it stands before the sun,
a shield, the shining god;
mountain and surf
I know shall burn
if it falls away.

39 Skol the wolf is called,
following the radiant god
to the protecting tree;
and the other is Hati,
he is Hrodvitnir's son,
following heaven's bright bride.

40 Out of Ymir's flesh
was the earth shaped,
and out of his blood the sea,
mountains from his bones,

trees from his hair,
and out of his skull the heavens.

41 And from his eyelashes
the helpful Powers girdled
Midgard for men,
and from his brain
were the stern-minded
clouds all shaped.

42 The grace of Ull
and all the gods,
is on whoever first grasps the fire,
because the worlds are open
for the Aesir sons,
when the cauldron is lifted up.

43 Ivaldi's sons
in days of old
shaped Skidbladnir,
the best of ships,
for shining Frey,
Niord's helpful son.

44 The ash Yggdrasil
is the noblest of trees,
and Skidbladnir of ships,
Odin of the Aesir
and of horses, Sleipnir;
Bilrost of bridges,
and Bragi of skalds,
Habrok of hawks,
and of hounds, Garm.

45 My face I have now raised up
before the sons of the victory-gods,
it will bring the desired rescue,
all the Aesir
shall come to
Aegir's benches for
Aegir's feast.

46 I am called Grim,
I am called Gangleri,
Herian and Hialmberi,
Thekk and Thridi,
Thund and Ud,
Helblindi and Har;

47 Sad and Svipal
and Sanngetal,
Herteit and Hnikar,
Bileyg, Baleyg,
Bolverk, Fiolnir,
Grim and Grimnir,

26

Glapsvid and Fiolsvid;

48 Sidhott, Sidskegg,
Sigfadir, Hnikud,
Alfadir, Valfadir,
Atrid and Farmatyr,
by no one name
I am called all the time
since I journeyed among men.

49 Grimnir I am called
at Geirrod's,
and Jalk at Asmund's,
and then Kialar,
when I drew the sled;
Thror at the Thing,
Vidur at battles,
Osci and Omi,
Jafnhar and Biflindi,
Gondlir and Harbard with gods.

50 Svidur and Svidrir
I am called at Sokkmimir's,
and I deceived the old Jotun then,
when I to Midvidnir's
mighty son
became the bane.

51 You are drunk, Geirrod,
you have drank too much;
you are robbed of much,
when you don't have my support,
or of all the *einheriar*
and Odin's favor.

52 Many things I have told you,
but you have remembered little,
your friends have deceived you;
a sword laying
I see of my friend,
covered all in blood.

53 An edge-weary corpse
Ygg will now have,
I think your life has passed;
the *dísir* were wrathful
now you can see Odin,
approach me, if you can!

54 Odin I am now called,
Ygg I was called before,
Thund was my name before that,
Vak and Skilfing,
Vafud and Hroptatyr,
Gaut and Jalk with gods,

55 Ofnir and Svafnir,
I think they seem to
all come only from me.

King Geirrod sat and had a sword on his knee, and it was half drawn. But when he heard that Odin had come there, he stood up and wanted to take Odin from the fire. The sword slipped out of his hand, with the hilt down. The king dropped to his feet and fell forward, and the sword stood through him, and he held his bane. Odin then left. And Agnar was the king for a long time afterwards.

27

# SKIRNIR'S JOURNEY

*För Skírnis*

Frey, Niord's son, had sat in Hlidskialf and looked into all the worlds. He saw into Jotunheimar, and saw there a beautiful maiden, as she was coming from her father's hall to the storehouse. This gave him great spirit-sickness.

Skirnir was the name of Frey's shoe-boy. Niord asked him to speak with Frey. Then Skadi said:

1 You should get up now, Skirnir,
and go to ask
to speak with our boy,
and ask about this,
with whom is the wise
inheritor very angry.

Skirnir said:
2 Ill words
your son will give me,
if I go to speak with the boy,
and ask about this,
with whom is the wise one
so very angry with.

3 You tell me this, Frey,
leader of the hosts of the gods,
so I will know:
why do you sit
along the length of the hall,
my lord, throughout the days?

Frey said:
4 Why should I tell you,
young boy,
my great sorrow?
Because elf-rays
shine on every day,
and yet not upon my desire.

5 Your desire
doesn't seem so very great to me,
that you to me, warrior, cannot tell;
because together as children
we were in days of old,
we should trust each other well.

6 In Gymir's courtyard
I saw walking
a maid very desirable to me;
arms shining,
and from them
all the air and sea.

7 More desirable to me
than to any other man,
young, in days of old;
Aesir and elves
do not want this man
to be united with her.

8 Then give to me the mare,
that will carry me through the dark,
a flickering flame to show the way,
and that sword,
which fights by itself
against the Jotun's family.

9 The mare I give to you,
to carry you through the dark,
a flickering flame to show the way,
and that sword,
which will fight by itself,
if the wise man carries.

Skirnir spoke with the horse:
10 It is dark outside,
I say we should go
over the damp mountains,
run over the land of men;
we will both come back,
or he'll take us both,
the very powerful Jotun.

28

Skirnir rode to Jotunheimar and into Gymir's courtyard. There were vicious hounds, and they were tied before the gate in the fence that was around Gerd's hall. He rode on, there was a herdsman sitting on a mound, and said to him:

11 You tell me this, herdsman,
while you sit on the mound
and watch over all the ways:
how I may converse
and come to the young girl
past the bitches of Gymir?

12 Which one are you: fey,
or have you already gone forth?
Without conversation
you shall always be with
the good maid of Gymir.

13 The choices are better
than just complaining,
for someone willing to die;
in one day
my whole lifetime was shaped,
and all my life was laid down.

14 What is that roaring din,
the howling I now hear
in our house?
The earth trembles,
and all before it
Gymir's courtyard shakes.

The handmaiden said:
15 A man is outside of here,
climbing off the back of a mare,
letting the horse seize the earth.

16 Ask him to come in
inside our dwelling
and drink the precious mead!
Though I think this,
outside of here is
my brother's bane.

17 What are you, an elf,
or an Aesir son,
or a wise Vanir?
Why do you come alone
over the raging fire,
looking for our household?

18 I am not an elf,
or an Aesir's son,
or a wise Vanir,
though I came alone
over the raging fire,
looking for your household.

19 Eleven apples
I have here, all of gold,
these I would to you, Gerd, give,
to pay for your favor,
that you might say Frey
is your least-hated one alive.

20 Eleven apples
I will never accept
for anyone's desire,
nor with Frey
through our lives,
will we both live together.

21 A ring I will give to you,
the one that was burned
with Odin's young son;
eight that are equally heavy,
drip from it
every ninth night.

22 A ring I will not accept,
though it was burned
with Odin's young son;
I have no want for gold
in Gymir's court,
I share in my father's wealth.

23 You see this sword, maiden,
slender, inlaid,
which I have here in my hand?
Your head will be chopped
by me off your neck,
unless you give your consent.

24 Suffer coercion
I will never do
for any man's desire;
though I get that
if you meet Gymir,
not slow to fight,
you two will want to battle.

25 You see this sword, maiden,
slender, inlaid,
which I have here in my hand?
Before these edges
the ancient Jotun will fall,
your father would be doomed.

29

26 I will strike you with a taming-rod,
and I will tame you,
maiden, to my desires;
you shall go there,
where the sons of men
will never see you afterwards.

27 On the eagle's hill
you shall sit in the morning,
looking out from the world,
looking towards Hel;
you will loathe meat
just as men despise
glittering serpents.

28 You will be a strange sight,
when you come out,
at you Hrimnir will gaze,
at you every creature will stare!
You will be more widely known
than the gods' watchman
as you gape from your enclosure!

29 Frenzied and shrieking,
frustrated and tormented,
your tears grow with the anguish!
You sit down,
and I will tell you
heavy torments
and two-fold grief.

30 Monsters oppress
you all of the day
in the Jotun's courtyard;
in the rime-*thurs*'s halls
you shall every day
creep without choice,
creep without hope of choice,
weeping for delight
you shall have in return
and nurse your sorrows with tears.

31 With a three-headed *thurs*
you shall always dwell,
or be unwed;
your senses seized,
disease wastes away at you!
You will seem like a thistle,
that is filled to the bursting point
at the end of the harvest.

32 To the forest I went
and to the green wood,
to get a great twig;
I got a great twig.

33 Odin is angry with you,
the foremost Aesir is angry with you,
Frey shall hate you,
incredibly wretched girl,
and you have obtained
the greatest wrath of the gods.

34 Hear this Jotuns,
hear this rime-*thursar*,
sons of Suttung,
the troops of the Aesir themselves:
how I forbid,
how I deny,
the girl to have merriment with men,
men to have merriment with the girl.

35 Hrimgrimnir the *thurs* is called,
who shall have you,
beneath the death-gate;
laborers there at the wood's roots
will give you goats' urine!
A better drink
you will never get,
maiden, of your desire,
maiden, at my desire.

36 "*Thurs*" I *ríst* on you
and three staves,
lewdness and insanity
and impatience;
I can *ríst* it off,
just as I *ríst* it in,
if this is necessary.

37 You are welcomed now, youth,
and take the frosty cup,
full of ancient mead!
Though I had thought
that I would never
love one of the Vanir well.

38 My errand
I will completely know,
before I ride home from here,
when you to a Thing
want the mature
desirable son of Niord.

39 Barri is the name,
that we both know,
a secret grove;
and after nine nights
there will Niord's son
take sport with Gerd.

Then Skirnir rode home. Frey stood outside and called to him and asked for tidings:

40 You tell me this, Skirnir,
before removing the mare's saddle,
and you go one step further:
what did you accomplish
in Jotunheimar,
yours or my desire?

41 Barri is the name,
that we both know,
a secret grove;
and after nine nights
there will Niord's son
take sport with Gerd.

42 Long is one night,
longer are two,
how will I endure for three?
Often a month to me
seems less
than half of a night of courtship.

31

# Harbard's Song

*Harbarðzlioð*

Thor was traveling from the eastern-way and came to a sound. On the other side of the sound was a ferryman with his boat. Thor called:

1 Who is that young boy
standing there across the sound?

2 Who is that old man
that calls over the bay?

3 Ferry me over the sound,
I'll feed you in the morning,
I have a basket on my back,
no meat could be better;
I ate at my leisure,
before I left home,
herring and oats,
I have been sated on these.

4 Early deeds
you take pride in;
you don't know what has happened:
your kinsmen are sad,
I think that your mother is dead.

5 What you said just now,
everyone would think
very important to know,
that my mother is dead.

6 Yet it doesn't seem
that you have three good farms;
barelegged you stand,
and dressed like a vagabond,
not even, do you have any breeches.

7 Steer the oaken-boat here!
I will show you the place,
and whose boat
are you keeping near the shore?

8 Hildolf he is called,
who asked me to keep it,

a warrior shrewd of counsel,
who lives in Radseyiarsund;
he asked me not to ferry robbers
or horse thieves,
only good men,
and those I know well;
say your name
if you want to cross the sound.

9 I would tell my name,
even if I was an outlawed murderer,
and tell all my lineage:
I am Odin's son,
Meili's brother,
and Magni's father,
the powerful warrior of the gods;
with Thor you are conversing here.
This will I now ask,
what are you called.

10 Harbard I am called,
seldom do I conceal my name.

11 Why would you conceal your name,
unless you have a quarrel?

12 Even if I had no quarrel,
with such as you are,
I would then protect my life,
unless I was fey.

13 A loathsome bother it seems to me,
to wade over the water to you
and wet my balls;
I will repay you, infant, for your
jeering words,
if I come over the sound.

14 Here I will stand

32

and ask you to come over;
you have found no one sterner
since Hrungnir's death.

15 This is what you now refer to,
that I fought with Hrungnir,
the stouthearted Jotun,
out of stone his head was made;
though I made him fall
and sink before me.
What did you do, Harbard?

16 I was with Fiolvar
all of five winters,
on the island,
that is called Algroen;
we could fight there
and cause corpses to fall,
put many to the test,
choose among the women.

17 How did you turn the girls to you?

18 We had lively women,
if they were compliant to us,
we had wise women,
if they were agreeable,
out of sand they
wound rope
and from deep valleys
dug the ground;
I was to all of them
superior in strategies,
I slept with the seven sisters,
and I had all their lust and play.
What did you do, Thor?

19 I dropped Thiazi
the very fierce Jotun,
I threw up the eyes
of Allvaldi's son
into the bright heavens;
they are the greatest mark
of my achievement,
all men have seen them since.
What did you do, Harbard?

20 Mighty tricks
I played on the dark-riders,
when I lured them from their men;
toughest of Jotuns
I think Hlebard was,
he gave me great twigs,
and I tricked him out of his wits.

21 You repaid his good gifts with evil.

22 One oak thrives,
another is cut,
each is to itself in such things.
What did you do, Thor?

23 I was in the east
and killing Jotuns,
women wise in evil things,
that came from the mountains;
great would the Jotun race be,
if they all lived,
nothing would man be
on Midgard.
What did you do, Harbard?

24 I was in Valland
and took part in wars,
I incited boars,
to never negotiate peace;
Odin has earls,
when in battle they fall,
and Thor has the thralls.

25 Uneven to distribute
would you be among the Aesir,
if you had that great responsibility.

26 Thor has sufficient strength,
but no heart;
with fear and faint-spirit,
you were stuffed in a glove,
and you didn't seem to be Thor;
then you didn't dare
in your fear
to sneeze nor fart,
because Fialar might hear.

27 Harbard the coward,
I would drop you into Hel,
if I could reach over the sound.

28 Why reach over the sound
if we aren't quarreling?
What did you do, Thor?

29 I was in the east
and was at the river,
when I was attacked
by the sons of Svarang;
they threw rocks at me,
but enjoyed little success,
and they had to come before me
asking for peace.

33

What did you do, Harbard?

30 I was in the east
and was conversing with someone,
I played with the linen-white one,
and had a tryst,
I made the gold-bright one happy,
the sport gave me pleasure.

31 Good things are gotten from girls.

32 Your help
I was in need of, Thor,
when I held the linen-white maid.

33 I would have assisted you
if I could have done it.

34 I would have trusted you then,
unless you betrayed my trust.

35 I am not a heal-biter
like an old hide-shoe in spring.

36 What did you do, Thor?

37 Women berserkers
I fought in Hlesey;
they had done the worst things,
deceiving all the men.

38 That was a shameful deed, Thor,
to make war with women.

39 They were she-wolves,
and hardly women,
they smashed my ship,
as I had put ashore,
threatened me with iron clubs,
and chased Thialfi.
What did you do, Harbard?

40 I was in the army,
that here prepared
to raise war-banners,
and redden spears.

41 You are now talking about
offering to wage war on us.

42 Then I will repay you for that
with a ring for the hand,
as arbitrators use,
those who would give us peace.

43 Where did you learn these
offensive words,
I have never heard
more offensive ones.

44 I learned them from the old men
that live in the forest at home.

45 You give cairns a good name
calling them the forest at home.

46 That is how I deem such things.

47 Your circling words
will bring evil to you,
if I decide to wade over the water;
loud as a wolf
I think that you will howl,
if you get a blow from the hammer!

48 Sif has a lover at home,
he is whom you want to meet,
then you will suffer the hardships
that you are due.

49 You say whatever your mouth wants,
it would seem terrible to me,
weak-spirited man,
but I know you lie.

50 I believe I tell the truth,
you are slow in your journey,
you would now be a long way, Thor,
if you traveled day and night.

51 Harbard the coward,
you have held me up too long.

52 Asa-Thor,
I never would have thought
a herder could thwart your journey.

53 I will give you advice now:
row your boat here,
stop squabbling,
meet the father of Magni!

54 Go away from the sound!
You cannot use the boat.

55 Now show me the way,
since you won't ferry me across.

56 Little to say,
long to travel,

a while to the stick,
another to the stone,
hold to the left-hand way,
until you arrive at Verland,
there Fiorgyn will
meet Thor, her son,
and show him the kinsmen's way
to Odin's land.

57 Will I get there in a day?

58 With toil and trouble
while the sun shines,
as I think it will thaw.

59 Our talk will now be shortened,
since you answer me with mockery;
I will repay your refusal to ferry,
if you meet with me again.

60 Go where the fiends can have you!

# The Lay of Hymir

*Hymisqviða*

1 Long ago, the gods of the slain
made hunt-kills
and were in the mood for drinking,
before they were sated;
shook twigs
and looked at the lots,
they discovered that Aegir
had ample provisions.

2 The rock-dweller sat,
merry as a child, before them,
much like the son of
Miskorblinda;
stared into his eyes
Ygg's son defiantly:
You shall for the Aesir
often make beer.

3 The Jotun was troubled by
the quarrelsome man,
decided to get even
with the gods he did;
he asked Sif's man
to bring him something,
"so that I can all of the ale
for you heat."

4 Could not, the mighty
glorious gods
and greatest Powers,
get one anywhere,
until trustworthy
Tyr gave Hlorridi
great advice
and said this:

5 Lying on the eastern side
of Elivagar
is the very wise Hymir,
at the edge of heaven;
my father has,
the moody one, a kettle,
very capacious,

a *röst* deep.

6 Do you know, if we can get
that water-boiler?
If, friend, deceit
is used to get it.

7 Traveled a long
day further on,
from Asgard,
until they came to Egil's.
He commanded his goats,
with magnificent horns,
to go to the hall
that Hymir owned.

8 The boy found a hag,
very loathsome she seemed,
for heads she had
nine hundred.
And another came,
all in gold, forward,
white-browed, carrying
beer to him:

9 Kinsmen of Jotuns,
I wish you two,
two full of spirit,
to sit under the cauldron.
My beloved is many times
stingy with guests,
and has an evil disposition.

10 But the misshapen one
was late to return,
the hard-counseling Hymir,
home from hunting.
Went into the hall,
ringing icicles,
on the man, as he came,
his cheek-forest was frozen.

11 Hail to you, Hymir,

in good spirits!
Now your son has come
to your hall,
he whom we have waited for
from long journeys.
Accompanying him is
Hrod's adversary,
the friend of mankind,
who is called Veor.

12  You see where they sit
under the hall's gable,
they are hiding,
a pillar stands before them.
The pillar stick broke asunder
before the Jotun's eyes,
and then in two
the beam broke.

13  Eight shattered,
except for one of them,
it was hard-forged,
whole from the beam,
They went forward,
and the old Jotun
laid his eyes
on his enemies.

14  Did not speak his
feelings well when he saw
the *gýgr*'s weeping-causer
coming across the floor.
Then were bulls
three taken up
all at once the Jotun asked
to be sent for boiling.

15  They were lightened
a head shorter
and to the cooking fire
afterwards brought.
They were food for Sif's man,
before he went to bed,
by himself all of
two of Hymir's oxen.

16  It seemed to him
the friend of Hrungnir
that Hlorridi was
very full.
We will in the evening
of another day be
with fished-food
that three can live on.

17  Veor said he would

row in the water
if the bold Jotun
gave him bait.
Go to the herd,
if you think you can,
breaker of mountain-Danes,
to seek bait.

18  This I expect
that you will find
oxen for bait
is easy to obtain.
The boy quickly
hastened to the forest,
there an ox stood,
all black, out front.

19  Broke off the bull's
—the *thurs*-bane did—
stronghold above
the two horns.
Your deed seems
much worse,
master of ships,
than if you had sat still.

20  Asked that the roller-goat,
the lord of goats did,
of the descendant of apes,
be rowed out farther;
but the Jotun
said he
had little desire
to row very long.

21  The great Hymir dragged,
moodily, whales
on one hook
two up at the same time;
and behind him in the stern
Odin's relative,
Veor, with skill
prepared his line.

22  Baited his hook,
the protector of men,
the worm's one bane,
with the ox head;
yawned at the hook
the one hated by gods,
the girdle underneath
all lands.

23  Boldly dragged
courageous Thor

the poisonous-looking worm
up on board;
struck with the hammer
the high-mountain of hair,
hideous, from above,
the wolf's close brother.

24 The reindeer-enemy loudly sounded
and the stony ground howled,
the old ways
of earth all at the same time.
Then sank
the fish into the sea.

25 The unhappy Jotun,
when they rowed back,
while Hymir was at the oars
did not speak;
he turned the rudder
to another direction.

26 You would do
half the work with me
if you to home a whale
brought to the farmstead,
or the floating-goat
of ours secured.

27 Hlorridi went,
grasped onto the prow,
took with the bilgewaters
the sea-steed up;
alone with the oars
and with the bailing-scoop;
he carried to the farm
the Jotun's surf-pig
and the woody ridge
he went over.

28 And the Jotun
about his strength,
accustomed to contentiousness,
argued with Thor;
he said no man was strong,
even though he rows in a way
that is strong,
unless he breaks the cup.

29 And Hlorridi,
when it came to his hand,
quickly tried to break
the glass on the steep-stone;
sitting he struck
at the pillar;
but it was brought whole

back to Hymir afterwards.

30 But then that woman,
the wife, taught him
the very loving-counsel
that she knew:
Strike it on Hymir's skull!
He is harder,
the food-heavy Jotun,
than every cup.

31 Harshly he rose from his knees,
the lord of the goats,
used all
of his Aesir-*megin*;
whole was the man's
helmet-stump above,
but the wine-vessel,
round, was cracked.

32 I know a great treasure
has been taken from me,
I see my cup
on my knee in pieces.
The man said these words:
I may not say
after this ever again,
you are, ale, heated.

33 This is for you to decide,
if the treasure comes
out of our
farm, the beer-ship.
Tyr tried
twice to move it,
stood both times
the cauldron still before him.

34 The father of Modi
took it by the rim,
and made it move
to the floor of the hall;
put it on his head,
Sif's man, the cauldron,
and at his heels
were the rings.

35 He had not gone far
before taking a look
behind him, Odin's son,
one time;
he saw out of the stones
in the east, with Hymir,
a troop of warriors coming,
with many heads.

36 He took from his shoulders
the towering cauldron,
he swung Miollnir,
murder-loving, before him,
and the rock-whales
he killed them all.

37 They had not gone far
before he lay down,
Hlorridi's goat,
half-dead before them;
the harnessed team-mate was
lame in its bone,
and this the mischief-wise
Loki had caused.

38 But you have heard this
—he that is
knowledgeable about the gods
shall tell it more clearly—
how from the rock-dweller
he got compensation,
he paid with both
his children for it.

39 The one great-of-strength came
to the Thing of the gods,
and had the cauldron,
that Hymir had owned;
and the holy ones
shall drink well
of ale at Aegir's
every flax-harvest.

# Loki's Gibe

*Locasenna*

Aegir, who is called by another name Gymir, prepared ale for the Aesir when he had obtained the great kettle, as was just told. To the feast came Odin and Frigg, his wife. Thor did not come because he was on the eastern-way. Sif was there, Thor's wife; Bragi and Idunn, his wife. Tyr was there, he was one-handed. Fenrir-wolf bit his hand off, when he was bound. Niord was there and his wife, Skadi, Frey and Freyia, Vidar, Odin's son. Loki was there, and Frey's serving-men, Byggvir and Beyla. Many were there, Aesir and elves. Aegir had two serving-men, Fimafeng and Eldir. There was shining gold raised up before the firelight. The ale served itself. There was a great place of peace. Men much praised how good the serving-men of Aegir were. Loki would not bear this, and so he killed Fimafeng. Then the Aesir shook their shields and shouted at Loki, and chased him away to the woods, and they went to drinking. Loki turned back afterwards and met Eldir outside. Loki said to him:

1 **Y**ou tell me this, Eldir,
before you one more
foot go forward:
what in here
do they have for ale-talk,
the sons of the victory-gods?

*Eldir said:*
2 Discussions about their weapons
and their readiness of fight,
the sons of the victory-gods;
Aesir and elves
who are in here,
no man has a friendly word for you.

*Loki said:*
3 I shall go
in Aegir's hall,
to see that drinking feast;
strife and hatred
I will bring to the Aesir sons,
and I'll mix mischief in the mead.

*Eldir said:*
4 You know this, if you go
in Aegir's hall,
to see that drinking feast;
accusation and slander

if you pour on the gracious Powers:
they will wipe it off on you.

*Loki said:*
5 You know this, Eldir
if with me you shall
quarrel with wounding words:
be rich
I would in answers,
if you spoke too much.

Afterwards Loki went into the hall. But when they saw who was before them, who had come inside, they all became silent.

*Loki said:*
6 Thirsty I come
to these halls,
Lopt, from a long way,
to ask the Aesir
to give me
a drink of the precious mead.

7 Why are you so quiet,
swollen gods,
are you incapable of speech?
A seat and a place

select for me at the feast,
or send me away!

*Bragi said:*
8 A seat and a place
select for you at the feast,
the Aesir will never do,
because the Aesir know,
who they should
bring their great-drink.

*Loki said:*
9 You remember that, Odin,
in days of old with me
you blended blood;
partake of drink
you would not do,
unless it was brought to us both.

*Odin said:*
10 Rise up then, Vidar,
and let the wolf's father
sit at the drinking-feast,
lest about us Loki
speaks reproachful-staves
in Aegir's hall.

Then Vidar stood up and poured for
Loki. But before be drank, he spoke
to the Aesir:

11 Hail to the Aesir,
hail to the Asynior
and all the most holy gods!
Except for that one of the Aesir
sitting further in,
Bragi, on the benches.

*Bragi said:*
12 A horse and a sword
I will give from my possessions,
and Bragi will give you a ring,
lest the Aesir you
repay with ill will,
and incite the gods against you.

*Loki said:*
13 Horses and arm-rings
you will always be
lacking in both, Bragi;
Aesir and elves,
those who are in here,
you are the most wary at war
and most fearful with shots.

*Bragi said:*
14 I know, if I was outside,
as I am now inside,
Aegir's hall to come,
your head
I would carry in my hand,
I would repay you for your lies.

*Loki said:*
15 You are bold on the seat,
you won't do as you say,
Bragi, the bench-ornament;
you would go away
if you saw anger,
in a brave woman's disposition.

*Idunn said:*
16 I ask, Bragi,
that you do this for your kin
and all adopted relations,
that you to Loki
do not speak reproachful-staves
in Aegir's hall.

*Loki said:*
17 You be silent, Idunn!
You I say of all women
are the most man-crazy,
since your arms you
laid, brightly washed,
on your brother's killer.

*Idunn said:*
18 To Loki I won't say
reproachful-staves
in Aegir's hall;
I calmed Bragi,
beer-merry,
I don't want you two to argue.

*Gefion said:*
19 Why you two Aesir
should in here
quarrel with wounding words?
Lopt knows that
he is playing
and he is loved by all creatures.

*Loki said:*
20 You be silent, Gefion!
This will I now mention,
how to fool your senses:
the white boy
gave you a precious ornament
and you laid your knee over.

*Odin said:*

21 You are insane, Loki
and out of your wits,
to take your anger out on Gefion,
because all men's *ørlög*
I think that she knows everything
just as fully as I.

*Loki said:*

22 You be silent, Odin!
You never know how
to apportion a battle with men;
often you give
to them what you shouldn't give,
to the faint-hearted, victory.

*Odin said:*

23 You know, if I gave,
to them what I shouldn't have gave,
the faint-hearted, victory:
eight winters
you were beneath the earth
a woman milking cows,
and there you bore children—
I thought that very effeminate.

*Loki said:*

24 And you spoke *seidr*
on Samsey,
and practiced as a *völva*;
in a *vitki*'s form
you traveled amongst mankind—
I thought that very effeminate.

*Frigg said:*

25 Your *ørlög*
should never
be spoken of before others,
what you two Aesir
engaged at in days of old;
always conceal your ancient fate.

*Loki said:*

26 You be silent, Frigg!
You are Fiorgynn's daughter,
and have always been man-crazy,
as when Vei and Vili,
you allowed them, Vidrir's wife,
both you took into your embrace.

*Frigg said:*

27 You know, if I had
in Aegir's hall
a boy like Balder,
you would not get away

from the Aesir sons,
and you would face fierce fighting.

*Loki said:*

28 And you want, Frigg,
for me to tell more
of my evil-staves:
I caused this,
that you will not see riding
again Balder to the hall.

*Freyia said:*

29 You are insane, Loki,
when you tell your
horrible loathsome-staves;
of *ørlög* Frigg
I think knows all,
though she doesn't speak of it.

*Loki said:*

30 You be silent, Freyia!
I know you fully and completely,
you are not lacking in faults;
Aesir and elves,
those who are in here,
have all been your lovers.

*Freyia said:*

31 False is your tongue,
I think that your mouth
cries out evil,
the Aesir are angry with you,
and the Asynior,
you will go home distressed.

*Loki said:*

32 You be silent, Freyia!
You are an evildoer
and blended with much ill,
since you with your brother
the blithe Powers found,
and then you, Freyia, farted!

*Niord said:*

33 That is a little-harm,
even if she had held her husband,
a lover or either of them;
the wonder is, the Aesir's coward
has come in here,
and he has bore children.

*Loki said:*

34 You be silent, Niord!
You were sent east
as payment sent to the gods;

Hymir's girl
had you as a urine-trough
and pissed in your mouth.

*Niord said:*

35 This is my compensation,
when I was long ago
as hostage sent to the gods:
then I got a son,
the one no man hates,
thought to be the Aesir's protector.

*Loki said:*

36 You stop now, Niord,
you should have your moderation!
I will not have you lie any longer:
with your sister
you got such a son,
but worse was expected.

*Tyr said:*

37 Frey is the best
of all bold-riders
in the Aesir courtyards:
he causes no maid to weep
nor any man's wife,
and loosens the fetters of everyone.

*Loki said:*

38 You be silent, Tyr!
You can never
carry well with two;
the best hand
I remember was given,
the one Fenrir tore from you.

*Tyr said:*

39 A hand I am wanting,
but you Hrodrsvitnir,
both our losses are unfortunate;
the wolf doesn't have it well,
he shall in bonds
bide for Ragnarok.

*Loki said:*

40 You be silent, Tyr!
It was your wife
she who had a son with me;
an ell nor a penny
you have never had for this
outrage, wretch.

*Frey said:*

41 I see a wolf lying
before the mouth of a river,

until the Powers are destroyed;
you will be like this next,
unless you now be quiet,
bound, bale-smith.

*Loki said:*

42 A deal in gold
you took Gymir's daughter
and you traded your sword;
but when Muspel's sons
ride over Myrkvid,
how you will fight then, wretch?

*Byggvir said:*

43 You know, if I inherited the lineage
of Inguna-Frey
and such a blessed seat,
fine as marrow
I would grind the harm-crow
and lame him in every limb.

*Loki said:*

44 Who is that little one,
that I see wagging its tail,
and snap-wise snapping?
At Frey's ears
you will always be
and clucking under the millstone.

*Byggvir said:*

45 Byggvir I am called,
and I am said to be eager by
all gods and men;
thus am I here proudly,
drinking with Hropt's kin
ale all together.

*Loki said:*

46 You be silent, Byggvir!
You never know how
to divide meat among men;
and under the benches
you don't want to be found,
when they are fighting.

*Heimdall said:*

47 You are ale-drunk, Loki,
so that you are out of your wits,
why don't you stop speaking, Loki?
Because excessive drinking
causes everyone
to not restrain their speech.

*Loki said:*

48 You be silent, Heimdall!

You were in days of old
laid down a loathsome life;
a muddy back
you will always have
and stay awake guarding the gods.

*Skadi said:*
49 You are easy-going, Loki,
you won't be such for long
playing with a loose tail;
because on a rock you shall
in your rime-cold son's
yarn be bound by the gods.

*Loki said:*
50 You know, if on a rock I
in my rime-cold son's
yarn am bound by the gods:
first and last
I was at the life-laying,
when we seized upon Thiazi.

*Skadi said:*
51 You know, if first and last
you were at the life-laying
when they seized upon Thiazi:
from my sanctuaries
and meadows shall
always come cold counsel.

*Loki said:*
52 Lighter in speech
you were with Laufey's son,
when you led me to your bed,
I will mention such things,
tell our unfortunate faults.

Then Sif went forward and poured for
Loki into a rime-cold cup mead, and
said:

53 Hail to you now, Loki,
and take this rime-cold cup
full of ancient mead,
I alone you should first
allow among the Aesir sons
to be flawless.

He took the horn and drank from it.

54 That you would be,
if you were such,
guarded and hostile to men;
only I know,
such as I think I know,

the lover other than Hlorridi;
and that was the evil-wise Loki.

*Beyla said:*
55 All the mountains shake,
I think that traveling
home is Hlorridi;
he will demand peace,
from they who insult here
all gods and men.

*Loki said:*
56 You be silent, Beyla!
You are Byggvir's wife,
and mixed with much misfortune;
a greater monster
has not come among the Aesir sons,
you are covered in shit, dairymaid!

There came Thor and he said:

57 You be silent, cowardly wight!
My mighty hammer shall,
Miollnir, take away your speech;
shoulder rock
I will drop from your neck,
and then your life will go.

*Loki said:*
58 Jord's son
has now come in here;
why are you so belligerent, Thor?
But then you won't dare
when you should fight with the wolf,
and he will swallow Sigfadir.

*Thor said:*
59 You be silent, cowardly wight!
My mighty hammer shall,
Miollnir, take away your speech;
I will throw you up
and on the eastern-way,
no man will see you then.

*Loki said:*
60 Your journeys in the east
you should never
speak of before men
since in a glove's thumb
you crouched, *einheri*,
and didn't seem like Thor at all.

*Thor said:*
61 You be silent, cowardly wight!
My mighty hammer shall,

Miollnir, take away your speech;
by my best hand
Hrungnir's bane will drop you,
so that your bones are broken.

*Loki said:*
62 I think I will live
a long life,
though your hammer threatens me;
hard leather straps
you thought Skrymir had,
and meat you didn't get for food,
and you starved—hail but hungry.

*Thor said:*
63 You be silent, cowardly wight!
My mighty hammer shall,
Miollnir, take away your speech;
Hrungnir's bane
will send you to Hel,
beyond Nagrind.

*Loki said:*
64 I spoke before the Aesir,
I spoke before the Aesir sons,
all of my thoughts;
but for you alone
will I go out,
because I know you'll fight.

65 Ale you prepared, Aegir,
but you will never
afterwards prepare a drink-feast;
all your possessions,
that are here inside,
flames will play over them
and burn you on the backside!

And after that Loki had hid in Franang's Falls in a salmon's form. The Aesir took him. He was bound with the entrails of his son Nari. But Narfi, his son, was a wolf. Skadi took a venomous worm and fastened it up over Loki's face. Out of it dripped venom. Sigyn, Loki's wife, sat there and held a hand-washing basin under the venom. But when the hand-washing basin was full, she took the venom out; and in the meantime venom dripped on Loki. Then he would jerk so much at this, that it then shook all of the earth; and that is now called an earthquake.

45

# The Lay of Thrym

*Þrymsqviða*

1 Ving-Thor was angry
when he awakened
and his hammer
was missing;
his beard began to shudder,
his hair began to shake,
Jord's son decided
to reach for it.

2 And these words he
said first of all:
You listen now, Loki,
to what I now say,
what no one knows
nowhere on earth
nor in the upper-heavens:
the Aesir's hammer is missing.

3 They went to the fair
Freyia's courtyard,
and these words he
said first of all:
Will you to me, Freyia,
lend your feather-shaper,
if I my hammer
might find?

Freyia said:
4 I would give it to you,
even if it was made of gold,
and I would hand it over
even if it was made of silver.

5 Flew then Loki,
the feather-shaper roaring,
until he came out of
Asgard
and he came into
Jotunheimar.

6 Thrym sat on a mound,
the lord of the thursar,
for his dogs

braiding gold-collars
and his horses'
manes trimming even.

Thrym said:
7 How is it with the Aesir,
how is it with the elves?
Why have you come
to Jotunheimar?
It is ill with the Aesir,
it is ill with the elves.
Do you have Hlorridi's
hammer concealed?

8 I have Hlorridi's
hammer concealed
eight *rastir*
underneath the earth;
no man can take it
back to its home,
unless is brought to me
Freyia as wife.

9 Flew then Loki,
the feather-shaper roaring,
until he came out of
Jotunheimar
and he came into
Asgard;
Thor met him
in the middle of the courtyard,
and these words he
said first of all:

10 What have you for a message
for your troubles?
Speak from the air
the great news!
Often sitting
tales fail,
and lying down
they deliver lies.

11 I have toiled
and have a message:
Thrym has your hammer,
the lord of the *thursar*,
no man can take it
back to its home,
unless is brought to him
Freyia as a wife.

12 They went to the fair
Freyia to find,
and these words he
said first of all:
Get dressed in your, Freyia,
bridal linens!
We shall drive you
to Jotunheimar.

13 Freyia was angry then
and snorted in disgust,
all the Aesir halls
trembled from it,
it cracked the great
Brisingamen:
You will know I am
man-crazy,
if I go with you
to Jotunheimar.

14 The Aesir at once
all assembled,
and the Asynior
all deliberated,
and on this decided
the mighty gods:
how they Hlorridi's
hammer would regain.

15 Then said Heimdall this,
the whitest of the Aesir—
he knows as much,
as the Vanir:
Dress Thor then in
bridal linens,
let him have the great
Brisingamen!

16 Let on him
keys dangle
and wife's-weeds
fall to his knees,
and on his breast
spread stones,
and pleasingly
top off his head.

17 Then Thor said this,
the strongest of the Aesir:
Me would the Aesir
call effeminate,
if I put on
bridal linen.

18 Then Loki said this,
Laufey's son:
You should not say, Thor,
these words!
The Jotuns would
set up farms in Asgard,
unless to you your hammer
comes home.

19 Then they dressed Thor in
bridal linens,
and in the great
Brisingamen,
let on him
keys dangle,
and wife's-weeds
fall to his knees,
and on his breast
spread stones,
and pleasingly
topped off his head.

20 Then Loki said,
Laufey's son:
I will go with you
as a handmaiden,
we shall drive
to Jotunheimar.

21 At once were the goats
driven home,
hurried into the harness,
they ran well;
mountains broke,
the earth burned with fire,
Odin's son drove
to Jotunheimar.

22 Then Thrym said this,
the lord of the thursar:
Stand up, Jotuns,
and cover the benches!
Now comes to me
Freyia to be a wife,
Niord's daughter
from Noatun!

23 Walking here in the yard

gold-horned cows,
all-black oxen,
to the Jotun's joy;
many treasures I have,
many necklaces I have,
only Freyia do I
appear to be lacking.

24 In the evening they
came together early,
and before the Jotuns
ale was brought;
ate one ox,
eight salmon,
all the delicacies,
those for the women,
Sif's man drank
three vats of mead.

25 Then Thrym said this,
the lord of the thursar:
Have you seen a bride
bite so keenly?
I haven't seen a bride
bite so broadly,
nor any more mead
drank by a girl.

26 Sat the all-wise
handmaiden before him,
and found words
for the Jotun's comment:
Freyia ate nothing
for eight nights,
she was so yearning to come
to Jotunheimar.

27 Bent under the veil,
desiring to kiss,
but he sprang back
the length of the hall:
Why are so terrifying
Freyia's eyes?
Her eyes seem to me
burning with fire.

28 Sat the all-wise

handmaiden before him,
and found words
for the Jotun's comment:
Freyia never slept
for eight nights,
she was so yearning to come
to Jotunheimar.

29 In came the poor
Jotun's sister,
the bride fee
she dared to ask for:
Let me have from your hands
red rings,
if you would get
my love,
my love
and all my favor.

30 Then Thrym said this,
the lord of the thursar:
Bring in the hammer,
to bless the bride,
lay Miollnir
on the maid's knee,
bless us together
by Var's hand!

31 Leaped Hlorridi's
spirit in his breast,
his thoughts grew determined,
when he recognized the hammer;
he dropped Thrym first,
the lord of the thursar,
and the Jotun's family,
all were slain.

32 He dropped the old
Jotun's sister,
the bride fee she
had asked for;
a resounding blow was her lot
for the shillings,
and a hammer blow
for many rings.
And so came Odin's son
to have his hammer back.

# Ⴀһє Ⴊ҂ꙗ of Volund

Nidud was the name of the king in Svidiod. He had two sons and one daughter; she was called Bodvild. There were three brothers, sons of the Finnar king. One was called Slagfid, another Egil, the third Volund. They skied and hunted deer. They came to Ulfdalir and made their house there. There was a body of water that was called Ulfsiar. Early in the morning they found by the waterside three women, who were spinning linen. Beside them were their swan-shapers. They were valkyries. There were two daughters of King Hlodver, Hladgud Svanhvit and Hervor Alvit, the third was Olrun, daughter of Kiar of Valland. They brought them home to the house with them. Egil took Olrun, and Slagfid Svanhvit, and Volund Alvit. They dwelled there seven winters. Then they flew to visit a battle and did not come back afterwards. Then Egil skied to look for Olrun. And Slagfid looked for Svanhvit. But Volund sat in Ulfdalir. He was a skilled man, such that men know, in ancient sagas. King Nidud took him captive, as it is told here.

1 The maidens flew from the south,
through Myrkvid,
strange young wights,
to carry out *ørlög*;
there on the water's edge
they sat to rest,
the southern women,
spinning precious linen.

2 One of them took
Egil into her arms,
the fair human maid,
the shining embrace;
another was Svanhvit,
wearing swan-feathers;
and the third,
their sister,
wrapped her arms around the white
neck of Volund.

3 Settled thereafter
seven winters that way,
but in the eighth
all had a yearning,
and in the ninth
they needed to leave;
the maidens yearned
after Myrkvid,

strange young wights,
to carry out *ørlög*.

4 Came there from hunting
the weather-eyeing marksmen;
Slagfid and Egil
the hall was found empty;
went out and in
and looked about.
Eastward skied Egil
for Olrun,
and southward Slagfid
for Svanhvit.

5 But only Volund
sat at Ulfdalir;
he struck red gold
with close-set gems,
he coiled all
the arm-rings well;
thus he was urged,
by his shining
woman, if she
came, to make.

6 Heard this Nidud,
the Niarar lord,
that alone Volund

49

sat in Ulfdalir;
at night warriors journeyed,
their chain-mail riveted,
their shields flashing
in the crescent moon.

7 Climbed out of their saddles
at the gable-end of the hall,
then they went in
along the length of the hall;
they saw there on bast
rings were strung,
seven hundred all together,
that the warrior had.

8 And they took them off
and they removed none,
except for one,
that they left off.
Came there from hunting
the weather-eyeing marksman,
Volund, traveling
from a long way.

9 Went to brown
bear meat roast;
brushwood burning high,
the very dry fir-wood,
wood dried in the wind,
before Volund.

10 Sat on the bearskin,
counted rings,
the elf prince,
missed one;
he thought that
Hlodver's daughter,
the strange young wight,
she had come back again.

11 He sat such a long time,
that he slept,
and he awoke
joyless;
he knew that on his hands
were heavy restraints,
and on his feet
fetters clasped around.

12 Who are the boars
that have laid
bast-ropes
and bound me?

13 Called out now Nidud,

the Niarar lord:
Where did you get, Volund,
elf prince,
our treasures
in Ulfdalir?

14 The gold was not there
on Grani's way,
I think our land is far from
the mountains of the Rhine;
I know that we more
treasures owned
when our family was whole
and was at home.

15 Hladgud and Hervor,
born to Hlodver,
Olrun was crafty,
Kiar's daughter.

16 She went in
along the length of the hall,
stood on the middle-floor,
in a calm voice:
He is not fit for a household,
he who came out of the forest.

King Nidud gave his daughter,
Bodvild, the gold ring, the one he
took from Volund's bast-rope. And he
himself carried the sword, that Volund
owned.

But the queen said:
17 He shows his teeth
when he is shown the sword
and he Bodvild's
ring recognizes;
the eyes are like
those of a shining worm;
cut from him
mighty sinews
and set him afterwards
in the sea-stead!

So was it done, that the sinews were
cut at the hollow of the knees, and
he was put on a small island that was
before the land, called Saevarstad.
There he smithed for the king all kinds
of precious objects. No man dared to
go to him except the king alone.

Volund said:
18 Shines Nidud's

50

sword at his belt,
that which I sharpened,
as perfectly as I knew how,
and I hardened it,
as I thought fitting,
it seems to me, the shining sword
is always carried far away,
I will not see it to Volund
brought in the smithy.

19 Now Bodvild wears
my bride's—
I won't get compensation for this—
red ring.

20 He sat, he did not sleep, always
and he struck with his hammer;
in order to make things
for Nidud.
Two youngsters came
to see precious things,
Nidud's sons,
at Saevarstad.

21 They came to the chest,
demanded the key-bearer
open it with ill intentions,
they looked in;
there were many precious things,
they seemed to the boys,
to be red gold
and precious.

22 Come alone you two,
come another day!
I will to you two let the gold
be given;
do not say it to the maids
nor the house-servants,
or any man,
that you will meet with me.

23 Early called
the man to the other,
brother to brother:
Go to see the rings!

24 Came to the chest,
demanded the key-bearer
open it with ill intentions,
they looked in;
cut off the heads
of the boys,
and under the fen-of-the-fetters
laid their feet;

and their skulls
under their hair,
he covered outside in silver,
presented them to Nidud.

25 And out of the eyes
precious stones
he sent to the cunning
wife of Nidud;
and out of the teeth
of these two
he struck breast-rings,
sent them to Bodvild.

26 Then Bodvild took
the ring that was praised,
it had been broken:
I dare not say this,
except to you alone.

Volund said:
27 I will better
the break in the gold,
so that your father
thinks it fairer,
and your mother
much better,
and yourself
the same.

28 He overcame her with beer
because he knew better,
so that she on the bench
was asleep.
Now I have taken revenge
for my harms,
all except one
malicious thing.

29 I am fortunate, said Volund,
that I came to my webbed-feet,
that from me Nidud's people
tried to take.
Laughing Volund
lifted into the air,
weeping Bodvild
went from the island;
grieving for her lover
and her father's wrath.

30 Outside stood the cunning
queen of Nidud,
and she went inside
along the length of the hall;
and he on the hall-fence

sat to rest:
Are you awake, Nidud,
Niarar lord?

31 I am always awake,
joyless,
I sleep very little
since my sons died;
cold is my head,
cold is your counsel to me,
now I wish that
I was able to converse with Volund.

32 Say this to me, Volund,
elf prince:
what was the fate
of my boys?

33 An oath you shall make to me first
on all of these,
on a ship's board
and on a shield's rim,
on a mare's back
and on a sword's edge,
that you will not torment
Volund's wife
nor my bride
be a bane to,
though I have a wife that you know,
and have a child
in the hall.

34 You go to the smithy,
the one you made,
there will you find the bellows
blood splattered;
I cut off the heads
of your boys,
and under the fen-of-the-fetters
I laid their feet.

35 And their skulls
under their hair,
I covered outside in silver,
sent them to Nidud;
and out of the eyes
precious stones
I sent to the cunning
wife of Nidud.

36 And out of teeth
of those two
I struck breast-rings,
I sent to Bodvild;
now Bodvild grows
big with child
the only daughter
of you both.

37 You could not speak words
that are more anguishing to me,
nor do I wish for you, Volund,
any torment;
there is no man so high,
that he can take you off a horse,
nor so hostile
that he could shoot you from below,
there where you dangle
with the clouds above.

38 Laughing Volund
lifted to the air
and unhappy Nidud
sat there afterwards.

39 Rise up, Thakkrad,
my best thrall,
you ask Bodvild,
the white-lashed maiden,
to go fair-dressed
to counsel with her father.

40 Settle this, Bodvild,
what was said to me:
were you together with Volund
on the small island?

41 This is so, Nidud,
what he said to you:
together with Volund
on the small island,
alone for a short time,
I never should have been!

42 He, I
did not know,
he,
I could not resist.

52

# The Tale of Alvis

*Alvíssmál*

1 **S**pread the benches
now shall the bride come with me,
home in my company;
rushing into marriage
it will seem to everyone;
we shall not rest until we are home.

2 Who is this creature,
why is your nose so pale,
were you with a corpse last night?
like a *thurs*
it seems to me you are,
you are not born for this bride.

3 Alvis I am called,
I dwell beneath the earth,
and my place is under the stones;
a wagon's value
I have come with,
no creature breaks solid vows!

4 I will break them,
because I for the bride
have the authority of the father;
I was not home,
when the vow was sworn,
the one given by the gods.

5 Who is this warrior,
who believes he has authority over
the fair glowing woman?
Vagabond
few will know you,
who has brought you rings?

6 Ving-Thor I am called
—I have wandered widely—
I am the son of Sidgrani;
without my consent
you shall not have the young woman
or get consent for marriage.

7 Your consent

I want to have quickly
and get consent for marriage;
I wish to have,
rather than be without,
the snow-white girl.

8 The maiden's love
you will have,
wise guest, to keep close,
if you from the worlds know
everything to say
know.

9 You tell me this, Alvis
—the fate of all creatures
you seem to me, dwarf, to know—
what is earth called,
which lies before men's sons,
in every world.

10 Earth it is called with men,
and with Aesir fold,
called ways by the Vanir,
green one by Jotuns,
by elves growing one,
called mud by the upper Powers.

11 You tell me this, Alvis
—the fate of all creatures
you seem to me, dwarf, to know—
what the heavens are called,
that bend around,
in every world.

12 Heaven it is called with men,
and coverer with gods,
called wind-weaver by the Vanir,
upper-world by Jotuns,
by elves fair-roof,
by dwarves dripping-hall.

13 You tell me this, Alvis
—the fate of all creatures

you seem to me, dwarf, to know—
what the moon is called,
that is seen by men,
in every world.

14 Moon it is called with men,
and ball with the gods,
called the spinning-wheel in Hel,
hastener by Jotuns,
and shiner by dwarves,
called by elves year-counter.

15 You tell me this, Alvis
—the fate of all creatures
you seem to me, dwarf, to know—
what the sun is called,
that is seen by men's sons,
in every world.

16 Sol it is called with men,
and sun with the gods,
called by dwarves Dvalin's deluder,
ever-glow by Jotuns,
by elves fair-wheel,
all-shining by the Aesir sons.

17 You tell me this, Alvis
—the fate of all creatures
you seem to me, dwarf, to know—
what the clouds are called,
that mix with showers,
in every world.

18 Sky it is called with men,
and shower-hope with gods,
called wind-floater by Vanir,
wet-hope by Jotuns,
by elves weather-*megin*,
called in Hel concealing-helmet.

19 You tell me this, Alvis
—the fate of all creatures
you seem to me, dwarf, to know—
what the wind is called,
that fares widely,
in every world.

20 Wind it is called with men,
and waverer with gods,
called neigher by great Powers,
screamer by Jotuns,
by elves noisy-traveler,
called in Hel squall.

21 You tell me this, Alvis

—the fate of all creatures
you seem to me, dwarf, to know—
what is the calm called,
that must lie,
in every world.

22 Calm it is called with men,
and laying with the gods,
called wind-end by Vanir,
excessive-warmth by Jotuns,
by elves day-soother,
called by dwarves day's refuge.

23 You tell me this, Alvis
—the fate of all creatures
you seem to me, dwarf, to know—
what the water is called,
that men row,
in every world.

24 Sea it is called with men,
and endless-layer with gods,
called waves by Vanir,
eel-home by Jotuns,
by elves layer-end,
called by dwarves deep-waters.

25 You tell me this, Alvis
—the fate of all creatures
you seem to me, dwarf, to know—
what is fire called,
that burns before men's sons,
in every world.

26 Fire it is called with men,
and flame with the Aesir,
called flickering by Vanir,
ravager by Jotuns,
and burning one by dwarves,
called in Hel hurrier.

27 You tell me this, Alvis
—the fate of all creatures
you seem to me, dwarf, to know—
what is wood called,
that grows before men's sons,
in every world.

28 Wood it is called with men,
and field-mane with gods,
mountain-seaweed by my people,
fuel by Jotuns,
by elves fair-limb,
called wand by the Vanir.

29 You tell me this, Alvis
—the fate of all creatures
you seem to me, dwarf, to know—
what is night called,
whom Nor birthed,
in every world.

30 Night it is called with men,
and darkness with gods,
called masker by great Powers,
unlit by Jotuns,
by elves sleep-joy,
called by dwarves dream-goddess.

31 You tell me this, Alvis
—the fate of all creatures
you seem to me, dwarf, to know—
what is seed called,
that is sown by men's sons,
in every world.

32 Barley it is called with men,
and grain with gods,
called grower by Vanir,
food by Jotuns,
by elves brew-staff,
called in Hel head-hanger.

33 You tell me this, Alvis
—the fate of all creatures
you seem to me, dwarf, to know—
what is ale called,
that is drank by men's sons,
in every world.

34 Ale it is called with men,
and beer with the Aesir,
called drink by Vanir,
clear-liquid by Jotuns,
and in Hel mead,
called drink-feast by Suttung's sons.

35 In one breast
I never saw
more ancient staves,
many lists
I said to deceive you:
you are up, dwarf, at dawn,
now the sun shines on the hall.

# Che Fjrst Lay of Helgj Hundjngsbane

*Title derived from subject matter. Poem follows the title "Volsungaqviða" (The Lay of the Volsungs). This lay marks the beginning of the heroic poems and begins with an unusually large capital.*

1 Early was the age,
when the eagle yelled,
the holy waters fell
from Himinfiol;
then was Helgi,
the stouthearted one,
Borghild bore him
in Bralund.

2 Night was on the homestead,
Norns came,
they who noblemen's
lives shape;
they decreed the troop leader
would be the most famous
and of Budlungs
thought the best.

3 They twisted with strength
the *ørlög*-rope,
the road to the fortress
in Bralund;
they arranged
the golden thread
and under the moon's hall
fastened the middle.

4 East and west they
fastened the ends,
the praiseworthy one would have
the land in between;
the kinswoman of Neri threw
to the northern region
one rope,
she said she'd hold it always.

5 One thing was distressing to
the Ylfings's kinsman
and the maid
who gave birth:

a raven said to a raven
—sitting on a high branch
in expectation of food—
I know something:

6 Standing in armor
is Sigmund's son,
one day old,
now day is coming;
sharp eyed
as a warrior;
he is a wolf-friend,
we should be cheerful.

7 The troops thought they saw
a Dogling,
said among the men
a good year has come;
the leader himself went
from the din of battle
to bring to the young
prince a noble-leak.

8 He gave Helgi a name
and Hringstadir,
Solfiol, Snaefiol
and Sigarsvellir,
Hringstod, Hatun
and Himinvangar,
a blood-worm was made
for the brother of Sinfiotli.

9 Then began to grow
in the bosom of his friends
the high-born elm,
shining bliss;
he repaid and gave
gold to his followers,
the king did not spare
the bloodstained hoard.

10 The prince let a short time
pass before battle,
until the troop leader was
fifteen winters;
and he let harsh
Hunding be slain,
who for a long time ruled
land and people.

11 Asked afterwards
of Sigmund's son
treasures and rings,
the Hunding's sons,
because they had to
repay the prince
for the robbery
and their father's death.

12 The Budlung did not let
compensation be done,
nor the kinsmen
get compensation at all;
he said they should expect
a great storm
of gray spears
and Odin's wrath.

13 The warlords went
to the meeting-of-swords.
they had set up
at Logafiol;
struck Frodi's peace
between the friends,
Vidrir's dogs went
greedy for the corpses of the slain.

14 The prince sat
when he had slain
Alf and Eyiolf
under Arastein,
Hiorvard and Havard,
Hunding's sons;
he had destroyed all of
the family of spear-Mimir.

15 Then a light shined
from Logafiol,
and from that light
lightning came;
they were under helms
at Himinvangar.
Their armor was
blood-splattered
and from the spears
rays stood.

16 Asked early in the morning
from out of the wolf-lair
the Dogling to the
southern *dísir*,
if they wanted to go home
with the warriors
when night came;
elms were clashing.

17 But from her horse
Hogni's daughter
—the shield-rim din had passed—
said to the prince:
I think, that we have
other business,
than with the ring-breaker
drinking beer.

18 My father has
his girl
promised to the grim
Granmar's son;
but I have, Helgi,
called Hodbrodd
a king as valiant
as a cat's son.

19 The troop leader will come
in a few nights,
unless you him challenge
to the battlefield
or take the maid
from the mild one.

20 You should not fear
Isung's bane!
There will be the din of combat
unless I see death.

21 Sent messengers
the all-sovereign one did then,
through the sky and across the sea,
to request an escort,
ample
Ogn's radiant light
he offered men
and men's sons.

22 Ask them to quickly
go to the ships
and for Brandey
be prepared!
Then waited the prince,
until there came
innumerable men

from Hedinsey.

23 And there on the beach
out of Stafnsnes
they slid the boats out
adorned with gold;
asked Helgi
of Hiorleif this:
Have you inspected
the blameless men?

24 And the young king
said to the other;
it would be long and difficult
to count off Tronoey
long-headed ships
under the sailors,
that were from Orvasund
traveling forth.

25 Twelve hundred
true men;
though in Hatun
twice as many,
the war-troops of the king;
the din of battle is expected.

26 So the steerer caused
the stem-tents to be down,
the mild man's
troops awakened
and the Dogling
saw the days edge,
and the king
hoisted up the tree
sewn cloth
in Varinsiord.

27 The oars were crashing
and iron clashing,
shield rims cracked shield rims,
the Vikings rowed;
went hurtling forwards
under the noblemen,
the praiseworthy one's fleet
far away from the land.

28 So was it heard,
they came together
Kolga's sister
and long keels,
as mountains and surf
were breaking apart.

29 Helgi asked to draw

the high sail higher,
at the wave-meeting
the crew did not Thing-lie,
when the terrible
daughters of Aegir
the stay-bridle-horse
wanted to capsize.

30 And they themselves
did Sigrun above,
brave-in-battle, protect
and their traveler;
turned with great force
out of Ran's hand
the king's gulf-beast
to Gnipalund.

31 So there in the evening
in Unavagar
the fair-decorated ships
did float;
and they themselves
from Svarinshaug
with troubled spirits,
explored the place.

32 The descendant of gods asked,
Gudmund, this:
Who is the land-lord,
the one who steers the troops,
and who baleful-host
brought to land?

33 Sinfiotli said
—slung up on the yard-arm
was a red shield,
the shield rim was made of gold;
he was sound-warder,
who knew to answer
and with noblemen
exchange words:

34 Say this in the evening,
when swine
and bitches you
draw to slop,
that you saw Ylfings
coming in the east,
yearning for battle,
to Gnipalund.

35 Hodbrodd will there
find Hogni,
the prince that never retreats,
in the middle of his fleet,

who has often
sated eagles,
meanwhile you at the hand-mill
kissed slaves.

36 You know few, troop leader,
old stories,
when you, the nobleman
hurl untruths at;
you have eaten
the wolves' delicacies
and your brother
you were his slayer,
often suckled sores
with a cold mouth,
have into a heap of stones,
everywhere-loathed, slithered.

37 You were a *völva*
on Varinsey,
a woman wise-in-schemes,
you spread lies;
you said no man
would you have,
warriors in armor,
except Sinfiotli.

38 You were harmful,
a witch, valkyrie,
awful, fearsome
with Alfadir;
the *einheriar* would
all fight,
headstrong woman,
for your sake.

39 Nine had we
on Sagones,
all wolves,
I was their only father.

40 You were not the father
of Fenrir's wolves,
you are eldest of all,
such as I remember,
not since you were gelded
before Gnipalund,
by a *thurs* woman
at Thorsnes.

41 You were Siggeir's stepson,
laid under the homestead,
accustomed to wolf-song
out in the woods,
from you came harm

of all kinds by your hands,
when your brother's
breast you pierced.
It made you famous
for atrocious deeds.

42 You were Grani's bride
at Bravoll,
with a golden bit, were
ready to run;
I had wearied you
by much riding on the course,
scrawny under the saddle,
a slope-backed cow.

43 You were thought a child
without breeding,
when you Gullnir's
goats milked,
and on another time
as Imd's daughter
in a tattered dress;
will you talk any longer?

44 Rather I want
at Frekastein's
to feed ravens
on your corpse,
than your bitches
feed slop
or give to gelded boars;
may fiends fight over you!

45 You were, Sinfiotli,
much better
doing battle
and gladdening eagles,
than using useless
words to taunt,
though ring-breakers
fight better.

46 To me good is not expected
from Granmar's sons,
though the princes were better,
speaking honestly;
they have proven
at Moinsheimar,
to have the spirit,
to battle with swords.

47 Powerfully they
let run
Svipud and Sveggiud
to Solheimar,

59

the dewy dale's
dark slopes;
Mist's sea trembled
where the boys went.

48 They met the prince
at the courtyard-gate,
said with hostile intent
the peacemaker had come;
Hodbrodd stood up
wearing a helm,
he considered the horse-rider
his family:
Why are troubled expressions
on the Hniflungs?

49 Twisted the sand here
the swift keels,
mast-ring harts
and long yard-arms,
many shields,
smooth-shaved oars,
noble troops of the prince,
cheerful Ylfings.

50 Went, fifteen
armies, upon the land,
though out in Sogn are
seven thousand;
lay here by the enclosure
before Gnipalund
blue-black surf-beasts
and ornaments of gold.
They are a mighty large
host, there,
now will Helgi
not delay the sword-Thing.

51 Bridled horses run
to the great-Thing,
and Sporvitnir
to Sparinsheid,
Melnir and Mylnir
to Myrkvid!
Let no man
sit behind,
they who wound-flames
know how to wield.

52 Bid you Hogni
and Hring's sons,
Atli and Yngvi,
Alf the old;
they yearn
to do battle,
let Volsungs
get a reception!

53 Swiftly then,
they came together
the gray points
at Frekastein;
always was Helgi,
the Hunding's bane,
first in the army,
there where men battle,
keen to fight;
so had the prince
a hard mood-acorn.

54 Came there out of heaven
helmeted wights from above
—the spear din increased—
they protected the prince;
then Sigrun said this
—wound-wights flew,
witch-steeds ate
on Hugin's barley:

55 Whole you shall, prince,
benefit of men,
descendant of Yngvi,
and content in life be,
you have dropped
the flight-averse
boar, the one who caused
the sailor's death.

56 And you, Budlung,
are suitable for both
red rings
and the mighty maiden;
whole you shall, Budlung,
be suitable to enjoy
Hogni's daughter
and Hringstadir,
victory and land
when the battle ends.

# The Lay of Helgi Hiorvardsson

*Untitled*

Hiorvard was called king. He had four wives. One was called Alfhild, their son was called Hedin; another was called Saereid, their son was called Humlung; the third was called Sinriod, their son was called Hymling. King Hiorvard had this binding vow, to have as wife she, whom he thought most promising. He heard that King Svafnir had a daughter fairest of all, who was called Sigrlin.

His jarl was called Idmund. Atli was his son, who went to ask Sigrlin on the king's behalf. He dwelled all winter long with King Svafnir. There was a jarl called Franmar, foster parent to Sigrlin; his daughter was called Alof. The jarl advised that the maid be denied, and Atli went home.

Atli, the jarl's son, stood one day in a certain grove; and a fowl sat in the upper limbs over him and heard that his men called the most promising women those whom Hiorvard the king had. The fowl chirped; and Atli listened to what he said. He said:

1 Did you see Sigrlin,
Svafnir's daughter,
fairest of maids
in the beloved homeland?
Though pleasing-looking
the wives of Hiorvard
seem to the men
in Glasislund.

Atli said:
2 Will you with Atli,
Idmund's son,
wise-spirited fowl,
talk some more?

The fowl said:
I will, if the Budlung to me
will sacrifice,
and I choose, what I wish,
from the king's court.

Atli said:
3 You can't choose Hiorvard
nor his sons,
nor the fair
army-leader's brides,
no man's brides,
whom the Budlungs have;
bargain well together!

That is the way of friends.

The fowl said:
4 A temple I will choose,
many stone sanctuaries,
gold-horned cattle
from the prince's farmstead,
if Sigrlin in his
arms sleeps
and willingly
accompanies the boar.

This was before Atli went away. And when he came home and the king asked him for news, he said:

5 Had hardship
and not the mission;
exhausted our horses
in the high mountains,
afterwards were
wading the Saemorn;
then was denied to us
Svafnir's daughter,
endowed with rings,
whom we wanted to have.

The king bid that they should go another time. He went himself. And

61

when they came up on a mountain, saw in Svavaland burning lands and much horse-smoke. The king rode from off the mountain to the land and took quarters by a river. Atli held watch and went over the river. He found a house. A great fowl sat on the house and kept watch and was sleeping. Atli hurled a spear at the fowl to kill it, and in the house he found Sigrlin, the king's daughter, and Alof, the old man's daughter, and had them both away with him. Franmar the jarl had an eagle's form, and was keeping them from the army with much magic.

Hrodmar was called king, the suitor of Sigrlin. He killed Svavakonung and had pillaged and burned the land.

King Hiorvard took Sigrlin and Atli to Alof.

Hiorvard and Sigrlin had a son tall and promising. He was silent; no name stuck to him. He sat on a mound; he saw nine valkyries riding, and one was most magnificent.

She said:

6 You will be late, Helgi,
to determine the fate of rings,
mighty apple-tree-of-combat,
nor the fate of Rodulsvellir
—the eagle screeches early—
if you are always silent,
though you have a hard heart,
prince, to prove.

7 How will you accompany
the name Helgi,
bright-faced woman,
since you offer advice?
Think well on all before
you decide!
I will not accept it,
unless I have you!

8 Swords I know lay
in Sigarsholm,
four fewer
than fifty;
one of them
is better than all,
the bale of battle-needles,
and wrapped in gold.

9 A ring is on the hilt,
courage is in the middle,
fear is in the point,
for they who get to own it;
lying on the edge
is a bloodstained serpent,
and on the handle-boss
an adder chases its tail.

Eylimi was called king. His daughter was Svava. She was a valkyrie and rode air and sea. She gave Helgi that name and protected him often afterwards in battle.

Helgi said:

10 You are not, Hiorvard,
a wise-in-council king,
spearhead of the troops,
though you are famous;
you let fire eat
the prince's settlements,
and grief they to you
did not give.

11 But Hrodmar shall
determine the fate of rings,
they which were owned
by our relatives;
that troop leaders has
little to live for,
thinks the dead
inheritance is his.

Hiorvard answered that he would obtain a body of men for Helgi if he wanted to avenge his mother's father. Then Helgi sought the sword that Svava directed him to. Then he and Atli went and killed Hrodmar and did many powerful-deeds. He killed the Jotun Hati as he sat on a certain mountain cliff. Helgi and Atli laid the ships in Hatafiord. Atli stood watch the first part of the night.

Hrimgerd, Hati's daughter, said:

12 Who are those men
in Hatafiord?
Shields are hanging
on your ships;
behaving boldly,
few I think do you fear;
tell me the name of the king!

Atli said:

13 Helgi he is called,
and you will never
cause harm to the prince;
iron-castles are
on the nobleman's fleet,
no hag may take us.

14 What is your name, said Hrimgerd,
overwhelmingly-powerful man,
what do men call you?
The troop leader trusts you,
he lets you in the fair
prow on the ship stay.

15 Atli I am called,
"fierce" I shall be to you,
I am most hostile to hags;
in the prow of the ship
I have often stayed
and tormented evening-riders.

16 What are you called,
corpse-greedy witch?
Name your father, hag!
Nine *rastir*
you should be farther down;
with conifers growing on you!

17 Hrimgerd I am called,
Hati is the name of my father,
he is the worst Jotun I know;
many brides
he took from farmsteads,
until Helgi chopped him down.

18 You were wary, witch,
before the prince's ships
and waited at the fjord's mouth,
drove the prince
as if you wanted to give to Ran,
if a sharp point hadn't pierced you.

19 Now you are deluded, Atli,
I say that you are dreaming,
your brows sink in frustration,
my mother
lay before the prince's ships,
I drowned Hlodvard's son.

20 You would neigh, Atli,
if you were not a gelding,
Hrimgerd is raising her tail;
the heart is further back
in you I think, Atli,

though you have a stallion's voice.

21 A stallion I would seem to you,
if you would try me out,
and I came ashore;
all of you would be lame,
if I was determined,
and your tail dropped, Hrimgerd.

22 Atli, come onto the land,
if you trust your strength,
and meet me in Varinsvik;
your ribs straightened
if you would, warrior, come,
if you in my clutches came.

23 I will not go,
before the men awake,
and stand guard for the prince;
it would not be unexpected to me,
if you came near us,
witch, up under the ship.

24 Awaken, Helgi,
and compensate Hrimgerd,
because as you cut down Hati;
one night
she can sleep beside the boar,
then her sorrows will be eased.

25 Lodin shall have you,
you are loathed by mankind;
that *thurs* lives in Tholley,
the very wise Jotun,
the worst of rock-dwellers;
for you he is a suitable man.

26 You would rather want her, Helgi,
who has been spying
earlier in the night with the men;
a very golden maiden
I thought she was very strong;
here she came ashore from the sea
and secured your fleet.
Only she is suitable
to stop me from being
the killer of the Budlung's men.

27 Hear me now, Hrimgerd,
if I compensate you for your grief,
you say everything to the prince:
was it one wight,
who saved the nobleman's ships,
or did more do it together?

28 Three nines of maidens,
though one rode out front,
white under the girl's helmet;
the horses shook,
off the stud's manes
dew dripped into the dale,
hail in the high wood;
thence comes the world's abundance;
all of what I saw was loathsome.

29 Look east now, Hrimgerd,
you have been struck by
Helgi's Hel-staves;
on land and on water
the prince's fleet is protected
and the prince's men the same.

30 Now it is day, Hrimgerd,
and you have been delayed
by Atli until your life's-end;
a harbor mark
you will seem ridiculous,
there you stand like a stone.

King Helgi was a very-good warrior.
He came to King Eylimi and asked
for Svava, his daughter. Then Helgi
and Svava exchanged vows and love
very much. Svava was home with her
father, and Helgi was on a military
expedition. Svava was a valkyrie the
same as before.

Hedin was home with his father,
King Hiorvard, in Norway. Hedin went
alone to his home from the forest Yule-
eve and met a troll-woman; she rode a
wolf and had serpents as bridles, and
asked to accompany Hedin. "No," he
said. She said: "You shall be repaid for
this at the oath-goblet."

In the evening it was time to make
vows. The sacrificial boar was brought
out front, men laid their hands on it,
and men made solemn pledges then
with the oath-goblet. Hedin made
a solemn vow for Svava, Eylimi's
daughter, the beloved of Helgi, his
brother, and regretted it much, so that
he went on the wild-path south on land
and met Helgi, his brother.

Helgi said:
31 Hail, Hedin!
Can you say if you know
new spells

from Norway?
Why are you, peacemaker,
driven from the land
and coming alone
to meet us?

32 A great crime have I
sought out,
I have chosen
the king-born
bride of yours,
on the oath-goblet.

33 Reproach not yourself!
It will be true
ale talk, Hedin,
for both of us;
the peacemaker had to me
appointed a combat in the sand,
three nights,
I shall come there,
I am in doubt
that I will come back afterwards;
then it may be good
that such is done, if it should be.

34 You say, Helgi,
that Hedin is
worthy of good from you
and greatest gifts;
it is more fitting
to redden your sword
than to give peace
to your enemies.

Then Helgi said that he had suspicions
about his death and that his *fylgia* had
visited Hedin when he saw the woman
riding the wolf.

Alf was called king, Hrodmar's son;
who had for Helgi marked the field in
Sigarsvellir in the nights' time.

Then said Helgi:
35 Rode a wolf,
as it grew dark,
that woman, who of him
asked for company;
she knew that
he would die,
Sigrlin's son,
at Sigarsvellir.

There was a great battle, and Helgi
took a mortal wound.

36 Helgi sent
Sigar to ride
after Eylimi's
only daughter;
asked to quickly
be ready,
if she wanted to meet
the troop leaders alive.

37 Helgi had me
sent here,
with you, Svava,
to speak myself;
the prince said you
wanted to meet,
before the high-born one
gave up his breath.

38 What happened to Helgi,
Hiorvard's son?
To me a cruel
harm has been caused,
if the sea has ruined him
or the sword has bitten,
those men I shall
bring injuries to.

39 Fell here this morning
at Frekastein
the Budlung, who was
best under the sun;
Alf was victorious
in everything,
though it
was unnecessary.

40 Hail to you, Svava!

You should fight your disposition,
in the world this will
be the last meeting;
the Budlung shows
blood down below,
I have been struck
near to the heart.

41 I bid you, Svava,
—bride, do not mourn!—
if you will my
words listen to,
that you with Hedin
rest
and the young prince
give your love.

42 I said this
in the beloved homeland,
when Helgi for me
chose rings:
I would not willingly
if the troop leader hadn't passed,
let an unknown boar
be in my arms.

43 Kiss me, Svava!
I will not come to
Rogheim to visit
nor Rodulsfiol,
before I have avenged
Hiorvard's son,
the Budlung was
best under the sun.

Helgi and Svava are said to have been reborn.

# The Second Lay of Helgi Hundingsbane

*Untitled*
*The stanza order of this poem is defective in the manuscript, but is given here in a more acceptable format. The original order is still reflected in the numbering of stanzas.*

Sigmund the king, Volsung's son, married Borghild of Bralund. They called their son Helgi, after Helgi Hiorvardsson. Helgi was fostered by Hagal.

Hunding was called a mighty king. After him was Hundland named. He was a great warrior and had many sons who were in battles. War and hostility was between King Hunding and King Sigmund; each killed the other's kinsmen. King Sigmund and his kinsmen are called Volsungs and Ylfings.

Helgi went and spied on the court of King Hunding in secret. Haeming, son of King Hunding, was home. And when Helgi went away, then he met a herdboy and said:

1 You say to Haeming,
that Helgi remembers,
whom in armor
the men killed;
a gray wolf
is in the house,
he who was thought to be Hamal
by King Hunding.

Hamal was called the son of Hagal. King Hunding sent men to Hagal to look for Helgi. And Helgi could not escape another way, but he took the clothes of a bondwoman and went to a mill. They searched and did not find Helgi. Then said Blind the bale-wise:

2 Keen are the eyes
of Hagal's slave,
that is not a peasant,
who stands at the mill;
stones crack,
the mill stand is falling down.

3 Now has a hard destiny
the warlord,
the prince shall
mill Welsh-barley.
It is more fitting
for those hands

the middle-piece
than a quern handle.

Hagal answered and said:

4 That is of little woe,
though the mill-stand thunders,
as the king's maid
moves the quern handle;
she sped forward
over the clouds
and dared to fight
as a Viking,
before Helgi her
made a captive of;
the sister she is of
Sigar and Hogni,
thus she has fierce eyes
the Ylfings girl.

Helgi came away and went on a warship. He killed Hunding the king and was then called Helgi Hundingsbane. He lay with his army in Brunavagar and had there *strandhögg*, and ate it raw. Hogni was called king. His daughter was Sigrun, she was a valkyrie and rode the sky and sea. She was Svava born-again. Sigrun rode to Helgi's ship and said:

5 Who caused to float
the ships by the bank,
where, warriors,
have you homes?
Why do you wait
in Brunavagar,
where do you desire
to make your course?

6 Hamal caused to float
the ships by the bank,
he has a home
in Hlesey;
waiting on a fair-wind
in Brunavagar,
east we desire to
make our course.

7 Where have you, ruler,
awakened battle
or fed the gaggle of
Gunn's sisters?
Why is your armor
blood splattered,
why under helms do
you eat raw meat?

8 Most recently opposed the
kinsmen of the Ylfings,
to the west of the sea,
if you desire to know,
where I took bears
in Bragalund
and to the eagle's family
fed with weapon-points.

9 Now I have said, maid,
why the quarrel happened;
thus I was on the sea
eating barely cooked.

10 War you reveal,
was before Helgi
Hunding the King
fell on the plain;
a battle was caused
to avenge relatives,
and blood streamed
on sword edges.

11 How did you know,
that we are they,
wise-mined lady,
avengers of the relatives?
Many are the keen
prince's sons

and are similar
to us kinsmen.

12 I was not far away,
spearhead of the troops,
yesterday morning
the prince's life ended;
though I saw the sly
son of Sigmund,
with corpse-runes
saying battle-spells.

13 I looked for you before then
on the longships,
when you were in the
bloody ship's stem
and in cold wet waves
did play;
now wants to conceal
the prince, from me,
but Hogni's maid
recognizes Helgi.

Granmar was called a mighty king,
who lived in Svarinshaug. He had
many sons: Hodbrodd, Gudmund
second, Starkad third. Hodbrodd was
at a king-meeting, he was betrothed to
Sigrun, Hogni's daughter. But when
she heard that, then she rode with the
valkyries on the air and on sea to seek
Helgi.
Helgi was then at Logafiol and had
surpassed the sons of Hunding. There
he killed Alf and Eyiolf, Hiorvard
and Hervard, and he was very battle-
weary, and sat below Arastein. There
Sigrun met him, and wrapped around
his neck and kissed him and told him
her errand, thus it is told in the ancient
*Lay of the Volsungs.*

14 Sigrun sought
the glad prince,
to take a home on Helgi's
hand she sought;
kissed and said to
the king under the helm,
that the king was
attractive to the woman.

15 She had already loved
with all her spirit,
the son of Sigmund,
even before she had seen.

16 I was to Hodbrodd

among the warriors betrothed,
but another boar
I wanted to have;
though I fear, troop leader,
my kinsmen's wrath,
I have my father's
dearest wish broken.

17 Hogni's maid did not
speak against the thoughts,
said she Helgi's
favor would have.

18 You need not be concerned,
for Hogni's wrath,
nor the ill disposition
of your kinsmen!
You shall, young maid,
live with me,
your family, good one,
I do not fear.

Helgi assembled then a great fleet of ships and went to Frekastein, and came upon a mortally dangerous storm. Then came lightning over them, and the flashing horses around the ships. They saw in the air that nine valkyries rode, and they recognized Sigrun. Then the storm abated, and then they came whole to the land.

Granmar's sons sat on a certain cliff, when the ships sailed to land. Gudmund leapt on a horse and rode to spy from the cliff near the harbor; then the Volsungs lowered sails. Then Gudmund said, as it was written before in *Lay of Helgi*:

Who is the troop leader,
that steers the fleet
and evil troops
brought to land?

Sinfiotli, Sigmund's son, answered,
as it is also written.

Then Gudmund Granmarsson said:
24 Who is this Skioldung,
who steers the ships,
showing war-banners
of gold before the prow?
It seems to me peace
is far from the forefront,
battle-red is cast

over the Vikings.

Sinfiotli said:
25 Here may Hodbrodd
recognize Helgi,
averse to flight,
in the middle of the fleet;
he has the possessions of
your kinsmen,
the inheritance of the Fiorsungs,
under his throng.

26 We should
at Frekastein
sit together
to settle the dispute;
it is a case, Hodbrodd,
to take revenge for,
we have the lower lot
long bore.

27 You will rather, Gudmund,
hold goats,
and a chasm
steeply climb,
have in your hand
a hazel-stick;
that you will find kinder
than the sword's judgment.

28 You, Sinfiotli,
are more fitting
to do battle
and gladden eagles,
than useless
words throw,
though the warlords
are bitter enemies.

29 Not expected by me goodness
from Granmar's sons,
though the princes are worthy
truth be said;
they have marked this
at Moinsheimar,
that they have the spirit,
to wield swords;
the warlords are
far too brave.

Gudmund rode home with the tidings of war. Then gathered Granmar's sons an army. Came there many kings. There was Hogni, Sigrun's father, and his sons Bragi and Dag. There was a great battle, and all Granmar's sons fell and all of the noblemen, except Dag, Hogni's son, got a truce and made oaths to the Volsungs.

Sigrun went to the corpse-place and found Hodbrodd coming upon death. She said:

19 Never will, Sigrun
   from Sefafiol,
   king Hodbrodd,
   fall into your arms;
   life is passing away
   —soon near the corpses,
   the gray-steeds of witches—
   for Granmar's son.

Then she met Helgi and was overjoyed. He said:

20 It is not to you all
   strange creature, given,
   though I say that the
   Norns wielded it;
   fell this morning
   at Frekastein
   Bragi and Hogni,
   I was their bane.

21 And at Styrkleifar
   king Starkad,
   and at Hlebiorg
   the sons of Hrollaug;
   I saw the ruler's
   grim-minded
   body fighting,
   the head was missing.

22 Lying on the earth
   nearly all
   your kinsmen,
   as corpses;
   you could not stop the battle,
   that was shaped for you,
   you are the strife
   of powerful men.

Then Sigrun wept. He said:

23 Be comforted, Sigrun!
   Hild you have been for us;
   Skioldungs couldn't fight destiny,
   I would now choose life,
   for the troops,

and may I still hold on to you.

Helgi took Sigrun, and they had sons. Helgi did not grow old. Dag, Hogni's son, sacrificed to Odin to avenge his father. Odin lent Dag his spear. Dag took Helgi, his in-law, at the place that is called Fioturlund. He ran through Helgi with this spear. There Helgi fell. And Dag rode to the mountains and told Sigrun the tidings:

30 Reluctant I am, sister,
   to say what grieves you,
   because I have under duress
   saddened my kinswoman:
   fell this morning
   under Fioturlund
   the Budlung, who was
   best in the world
   and on warlords'
   necks stood.

31 Should all your
   oaths be cut,
   that to Helgi
   you had given,
   by the bright
   Leipt's waters
   and cold-wet
   Unn's stone.

32 The ship will not glide
   under your direction,
   though a favorable wind
   lays behind you;
   the mare will not run
   under your direction,
   though your enemies
   move to take you.

33 The sword will not bite,
   that you wield,
   except at yourself
   singing over your head.
   On you is the revenge for
   Helgi's death,
   if you were a wolf
   out in the woods,
   wanting for riches
   and all pleasures,
   you would have no meat
   except the corpses you gorge on.

Dag said:

34 You are insane, sister,
and out of your wits,
on your brother you
ask for misfortune;
Odin alone wielded
all this evil,
because with your relatives
he brought strife-runes.

35 Your brother offers
red rings,
all of Vandilsve
and Vigdalir;
you can have half the homestead
to repay harms,
ring-adorned bride
and your sons!

36 I will not sit so fortunate
at Sefafiol,
neither early nor at night
will I desire that life,
unless on the praised one's troops
light is thrown,
running under the prince
Vigblaer comes here,
accustomed to the golden-bit,
so I might welcome the prince.

37 Helgi has so
terrified
all his enemies
and their kinsmen,
as before the wolf
running in fear
the goats from the mountain,
full of terror.

38 So was Helgi
out of the warlords
as a beautifully-shaped
ash out of the thorn-bushes,
and as a fawn,
slinging dew,
who is over
all animals
and horns glow
against heaven itself.

A mound was made for Helgi. And when he came to Valholl, then Odin asked him to rule over all with him.

Helgi said:
39 You shall, Hunding,
for every man

get a foot-bath
and kindle a fire,
bind the wounds,
tend the horses,
give slop to the swine,
before you go to sleep.

Sigrun's handmaiden went in the evening near Helgi's mound and saw that Helgi rode into the mound with many men.

The handmaiden said:
40 What is this deception,
that I think I see,
or is it Ragnarok,
and dead men ride?
Are you horses
urging with points,
and are the warlords
given back to the world?

41 This is not deception
that you think you see,
nor the end of the age,
though you look upon us,
though we our horses
urge with points,
nor are the warlords
given back to the world.

Homeward went the handmaiden and said to Sigrun:

42 Go out, Sigrun,
from Sefafiol,
if you the army protector
desire to meet;
the mound is opened up,
Helgi is coming;
battle-traces bleed,
the Dogling bids thee,
that you wound-drops
should staunch.

Sigrun went in the mound to Helgi and said:

43 Now I am so pleased
at our meeting
just as the ravenous
hawks of Odin,
when they know of slaughter,
warm meat,
or dew-colored

edge of day see.

44 First I want to kiss
the dead king,
before your bloody
mail shirt is cast aside;
your hair, Helgi,
is full of rime,
the prince is all
corpse-dew covered,
cold and wet are the hands
of Hogni's in-law;
how shall I, Budlung, this
attain a remedy for?

45 You caused, Sigrun
from Sefafiol,
Helgi to be
harm-dew covered;
you grieve, gold-adorned one,
grim tears,
sun-bright southerner,
before you go to sleep;
each falls bloody
on the prince's breast,
cold and wet, searing,
swollen with grief.

46 We shall drink
precious liquor,
though we have lost
our beloved land;
no man shall
say a mourning-lay,
though on my breast
mortal wounds appear;
now is the bride
dwelling in the mound,
the praiseworthy one's bride
is beside the troops.

Sigrun prepared a bed in the mound.

47 Here I have for you, Helgi,
made a resting-place,
free from anguish,
Ylfings kinsman,
I will in your embrace,
troop leaders, sleep,
as I with the praiseworthy one
did in life.

48 Now I say nothing
is unexpected,
late nor early

at Sefafiol,
that you in arms
unliving sleep,
white one, in the mound,
Hogni's daughter,
and you are quick,
and born to a king.

49 It is time for me to ride
reddened roads,
let pale horse
tread the flight path;
I go west to the
wind-helm's bridge,
before Salgofnir
awakens the host of victory.

Then Helgi rode off with his troops; and they went home to the homestead. The next evening Sigrun let the handmaiden hold guard at the mound. And at day-setting, Sigrun came to the mound...

She said:
50 By now would have come,
if he intended to come,
Sigmund's son,
from Odin's hall;
I say thoughts of prince
wanting are turning gray,
on ash-limbs are
eagles sitting
and all people drive
to the dream-Thing.

51 You should not be so insane,
to go alone,
woman of the Skioldungs,
to the house of the dead;
they are powerful,
much more at night
the dead villains, maiden,
than in daylight.

Sigrun was short-of-life from harm and grief.

It was believed in olden times that men were reborn, but that is now called a crone-error. Helgi and Sigrun were said to have been reborn. He was then called Helgi Haddingiascadi, and she Kara, Halfdan's daughter, as it is said in *Kara's Song*, and she was a valkyrie.

# Che Death of Sinfiotli

*Frá dauða Sinfiötla*
*Ellipses mark where two blank spaces were left in the text.*

Sigmund, Volsung's son, was king in France. Sinfiotli was his eldest son, another was Helgi, a third was Hamund. Borghild, the wife of Sigmund, had a brother, who was called ... . And Sinfiotli, her stepson, and ... both asked after one woman, and for this reason Sinfiotli killed him. And when he came home, then Borghild bid him away, but Sigmund offered her compensation-money, and advised her to accept it. But at the funeral feast Borghild brought the ale. She took poison, a great horn full, and brought it to Sinfiotli. But he saw in the horn; he discerned that poison was in it, and spoke to Sigmund: "Cloudy is the drink, great-grandfather." Sigmund took the horn and drank of it. Such was it said that Sigmund was so hardy that poison could not harm him outside or inside. And all his sons could stand poison on the outside of their skin. Borghild brought another horn to Sinfiotli, and bid him drink, and it went all the same as before. And the third time she brought him a horn, and with it insults, if he did not drink of it. He spoke the same as before with Sigmund. He said: "Then let your moustache strain it, son!" Sinfiotli drank and was immediately killed.

Sigmund carried him a long way in his arms and came to a certain fjord, narrow and long, and was there a little ship and a man in it. He offered to Sigmund to take him over the fjord. But when Sigmund brought the body onto the ship, then the boat was loaded. The man said that Sigmund should go around the inside of the fjord. The man pushed the ship out and immediately vanished.

King Sigmund dwelled a long time in Denmark at Borghild's domain, after that he took her as wife. Then Sigmund went south to France, to the dominion that he had there. Then he took Hiordis as wife, King Eylimi's daughter. Their son was Sigurd. King Sigmund fell in battle before Hunding's sons. And Hiordis was given in marriage then to Alf, son of King Hialprek. Sigurd grew up there in his childhood.

Sigmund and all his sons were foremost of all men in strength and stature and spirit and all accomplishments. Though Sigurd was foremost of them all, and he is called by all men in old traditions greatest of all men and stateliest of warrior-kings.

# Gripir's Prophecy

## *Untitled*

Gripir was the name of Eylimi's son, the brother of Hiordis. He ruled lands and was of all men wisest and most prophetic. Sigurd rode alone and came to Gripir's hall. Sigurd was easy to recognize. He met a man and spoke to him outside the hall; his name was Geitir. Then Sigurd spoke these words and asked:

1 Who lives here
in this fortress,
who is the people's-king
named by the thanes?

Gripir he is called,
the great man,
who firmly rules
earth and thanes.

2 Is the wise king
home in the land,
will the prince with me
come to speak?
It is necessary to speak for
the man who is unknown,
I want to immediately
meet Gripir.

3 This will the glad king
ask Geitir:
who this man is,
who asks to speak to Gripir?

Sigurd I am called,
born to Sigmund,
and Hiordis is
the prince's mother.

4 Then Geitir went
to say to Gripir:
There is a man here outside,
unknown, coming;
he is noble-looking
in appearance,
who wants, troop leader,
to meet with you.

5 Went out of the dwelling,
the warriors' leader,
and hailed well
the prince who had come:
You are welcome here, Sigurd,
it was proper earlier,
and you, Geitir, take
Grani to yourself!

6 They began to speak
and chat on many things,
when the wise-in-counsel
warriors met.
Say to me, if you know,
mother's-brother:
how will Sigurd's
life turn?

7 You will be of men
mightiest under the sun
and highest born
of every boar,
generous of gold,
and stingy of flight,
noble in appearance,
and prophetic in words.

8 You speak, just king,
completely, and I ask,
wisely, to Sigurd,
if you think you see:
What will first be done
of my destiny,
when I am out of the courtyard
of yours gone.

9 First you will, troop leader,

avenge your father
and for Eylimi
avenge all harms;
you will the hard
Hunding's sons,
boldly, kill,
you will have victory.

10 You speak, noble king,
kinsman, to me,
more wisely yet,
as we friendly converse:
Do you see Sigurd's
bold deed before him,
those surpassing the highest
under heaven's quarter?

11 You alone will slay
the glittering serpent,
the greedy one that lies
on Gnitaheid;
you will both
be the killer
of Regin and Fafnir,
says Gripir rightly.

12 Wealth will be sufficient,
if I am so strong
in battle with the men,
as you say is certain;
consider the path
and speak longer:
what more will be
in my life?

13 You will find
Fafnir's lair
and take up
a fair treasure,
load the gold
on Grani's shoulder;
you will ride to Giuki's
a combat-ready prince.

14 But you shall, king
of discerning-counsel,
to the high-minded boar
say more:
A guest I am of Giuki,
and I will go thence:
what more will be
in my life?

15 Sleeping on the mountain
the troop leaders's daughter,

bright, in armor,
after Helgi's death;
you will cut
with the sharp sword,
*ríst* the armor
with Fafnir's bane.

16 The armor is broken,
the bride begins to speak,
who has been awakened
the wife from her sleep;
what will the woman then
say to Sigurd,
what will the destiny
of the troop leader be?

17 She will to you powerful
runes teach,
completely, those men
want to possess,
and men's tongues
to speak all,
healing with leeches;
you will live whole, king!

18 Now that is concluded,
the lore is learned,
and I am away thence,
ready to ride;
consider the path
and speak longer:
what more will be
in my life?

19 You will visit
Heimir's dwelling
and be the glad
guest of the people's-king;
that is over, Sigurd,
what I knew before,
but of such you should not further
question Gripir.

20 Now sorrow takes hold of me,
the words that you speak,
because you see ahead,
troop leader, longer;
you know too much
anguish for Sigurd,
although you, Gripir, of that
are unwilling to say.

21 Lays the youth
of your life
clearly before me

74

to look after;
I am not rightly
reckoned wise-in-counsel,
nor prophetic,
that is all, that I know.

22 I know no man
on the earth,
that sees more
farther than you, Gripir;
you shall not conceal,
though it is loathsome,
or harm is prepared
in my circumstances.

23 Without shame
your life is laid,
you allow, noble one, that,
prince, to be accepted!
Because up will,
as men live,
bidder of spear-showers,
your name be.

24 This I think is worst,
to be leaving,
Sigurd from the troop leader,
as it is done;
you show me the path
—laid all the way before you—
famous one, to me, if you will,
my mother's-brother.

25 Now I shall to Sigurd
speak clearly,
since my prince
compels this;
I know for certain
what is not a lie:
one day for you
death is predetermined.

26 I do not want the wrath
of the mighty people's-king,
good advice, rather,
from Gripir, I would get;
now will I know clearly,
though it is unpleasant:
what for Sigurd is visible
at hand?

27 A woman is at Heimir's,
fair in appearance
—Brynhild she
is named by men—

the daughter of Budli,
and the dear king,
the stern-minded man,
Heimir, has raised.

28 What is this to me,
though the maid is
fair in appearance,
raised at Heimir's?
That you shall, Gripir,
completely say,
because you see all
*ørlög* before me.

29 She will rob you
of most of your delight,
the fair in appearance
foster child of Heimir;
you will not dream nor sleep,
nor judge cases,
you will not notice anyone,
unless you see the girl.

30 What comfort will be
laid for Sigurd?
You say, Gripir, that,
if you think you see it;
will I the maid
keep for a bride price,
the fair
troop leaders's daughter?

31 You two will all
oaths swear,
very bindingly,
few will you hold onto;
when you have been Giuki's
guest one night,
you will not know the wise
Heimir's foster child.

32 What is this, Gripir,
that you speak about for me?
See you fickleness
in the prince's character?
When I shall with the maid
tear up words,
who all my spirit
I thought loved.

33 You will be, prince,
deceived by another,
Grimhild will
counsel atonement;
she will offer you

the bright-hair girl,
her daughter,
she will drag upon the prince.

34 Will I then with Gunnar
be related by marriage
and Gudrun
go to have?
Well-married then
the troop leader will be,
if sorrowful repentance
is not grieving me.

35 You will Grimhild
completely deceive,
she will Brynhild
urge you to ask in marriage
to the hand of Gunnar,
the Goths' leader;
you immediately promise to go
for the troop leaders's mother.

36 Misfortune is at hand,
I can see that,
completely astray
are the decisions of Sigurd,
if I shall the famous
maiden ask in marriage
to another's hand,
the one I love well.

37 All will
make oaths,
Gunnar and Hogni,
and you prince, third,
because exchanged appearances,
on the road,
Gunnar and you;
Gripir does not lie.

38 What does that mean?
Why should we exchange
looks and actions
on the road?
Treachery will there
accompany it,
all with hostility:
and you tell it, Gripir!

39 You will have the look of Gunnar
and his bearing,
your eloquence
and *megin*-bearing;
you will betroth yourself
to the aspiring

foster child of Heimir,
nothing will be before this.

40 This is thought worst,
evil I will be called,
Sigurd, with warriors,
as it is so done;
I do not want
to deceptively bait
for the boar the bride,
whom I know is best.

41 You will rest,
spear-point of the army,
famous one, near the maid,
as if she was your mother;
you will be uppermost
while men live,
prince of the people,
you will be named.

42 The good wife will
Gunnar have,
the famous one, among men
—say this to me, Gripir!—
though for three nights
the thane's bride has near me,
resolute in spirit, slept?
Such is an example.

43 The nuptials will together
both be drunk,
Sigurd's and Gunnar's,
in Giuki's halls;
when likenesses are exchanged,
as you come home,
each will then have
his spirit.

44 How will pleasure
be afterwards
between the in-laws?
Say this to me, Gripir!
Will Gunnar
have all the pleasure
after this occurs,
or me myself?

45 Remember your oaths,
though you are silent,
you love Gudrun
to have good;
and Brynhild thinks,
the bride ill-given,
the woman will find a way

to get revenge.

46 What will in compensation
the bride take,
since I have deceptively
treated the woman?
The woman has from me
sworn oaths,
none fulfilled,
and little satisfaction.

47 She will to Gunnar
completely say,
that you did not
keep the oaths faithfully,
the ones the noble king
with all his spirit,
Giuki's heir,
trusted in the prince.

48 What is this, Gripir?
You are speaking about me!
Will I be true
to the sagas?
Or lie about me,
the glorious woman,
and herself?
You tell, Gripir, that!

49 With wrath will
the powerful bride be with you,
in deep sorrow will not
treat you very well;
you will not with the good one
repay injuries,
though the wife of the king

uses bait.

50 Will the wise Gunnar
be provoked by her,
Guthorm and Hogni,
afterwards?
Will Giuki's sons
on me, their relative,
redden edges?
And you say this, Gripir!

51 Then is Gudrun
grim of heart,
when her brothers
cause your death,
and there will be no
happiness afterwards
to the wise wife;
Grimhild causes this.

52 This shall comfort you,
spear-point of the army,
this good-luck will be laid
on the prince's life:
a mightier man will not
come to earth,
under the sun's seat,
than you, Sigurd, are thought.

53 We part with a hail!
What is shaped cannot be denied,
now you have, Gripir, well
done, as I asked;
quickly you would have
said more beautifully
my life,
if you could have done so.

# REGIN'S TALE

*Untitled*

Sigurd went to Hialprek's stud and chose one of the horses, who afterwards was called Grani. Then Regin came to Hialprek, Hreidmar's son. He was a very skilled man, and of dwarven stature; he was wise, grim, and much-knowing. He offered to foster Sigurd and instruct and love him much. He told Sigurd about his forefathers and these events, that Odin and Hoenir and Loki had come to Andvari's Falls; in these falls was a multitude of fish. A certain dwarf was called Andvari, he was for a long time in a pike's likeness and got his meat that way. Otr our brother is called, said Regin, who often goes in the falls in an otter's likeness. He took a salmon and sat on the river bank and ate with closed eyes. Loki struck him with a stone to kill him. The Aesir thought this was a happy thing and flayed the skin from the otter. That same evening they sought lodging with Hreidmar and showed their kill. Then we bound their arms and ordered them to loosen-their-lives by filling the otter skin with gold and covering the outside also with red gold. Then they sent Loki to procure the gold. He went to Ran and took her net and went to Andvari's Falls and cast the net before the pike; and he leapt into the net. Then Loki said:

1 Who is this fish
  that runs in the water?
  Who doesn't know caution?
  Your head
  you can loosen from Hel,
  find me the river's flame!

2 Andvari I am called,
  Oin my father is called,
  much I have journeyed in the falls;
  a wretched Norn
  shaped in days of old,
  that I shall in water wade.

3 Say this, Andvari, Loki said,
  if you want to have
  a life in people's halls:
  what compensation is gotten
  by men's sons,
  if they fight with words?

4 An awful-payment is gotten
  by men's sons,
  they will wade Vadgelmir;
  untrue words,
  when one lies to another,

for a long time stay with the limbs.

Loki saw all the gold that Andvari had. And when he had raised up the gold, then he had afterwards one ring, and Loki took that from him. The dwarf went onto a rock and spoke:

5 That gold shall,
  what Gust owned,
  two brothers,
  be the bane of,
  and princes
  eight will have strife;
  my treasure will
  no man enjoy.

The Aesir readied the treasure for Hreidmar and filled up the otter's skin and raised its feet. Then the Aesir heaped gold up and covered it. When that was done, Hreidmar went forward and saw one gray hair, and asked it to be covered. Then Odin drew forth Andvari's Gift and covered the hair.

6 Your gold is prepared, Loki said,
and you have payment
for your head greatly;
for your sons
are no blessings shaped,
it will be the bane of both.

Hreidmar said:
7 Gifts you gave,
you did not give love-gifts,
you did not give wholeheartedly,
your lives
would have been taken,
if I knew of this danger before.

8 But it is worse
—I think I know this—
kinsmen's strife is destructive;
the boars are not born
that I think
this hate is intended for.

9 Red gold, said Hreidmar,
I think I will have rule over,
as long as I live;
your threat
does not threaten my life,
and you go home from here!

Fafnir and Regin craved Hreidmar's kin-compensation for Otr, their brother. He said no to this. And Fafnir put a sword into Hreidmar, his father, as he slept. Hreidmar called to his daughter:

10 Lyngheid and Lofnheid
know that my life is leaving!
Much is that which compels thee.

Lyngheid answered:
Few sisters will,
though missing a father,
avenge harm on a brother.

Hreidmar said:
11 You'll have a daughter,
wolf-hearted woman,
if you do not get a son
with a prince;
give the maid to a man,
if in great need!
Then will their son
avenge your wrongs.

Then Hreidmar died. And Fafnir took all the gold. Then Regin asked to have his inheritance from his father; but Fafnir would not pay it. Then Regin sought counsel with Lyngheid, his sister, for how he should bring home his father's inheritance.

She said:
12 Speak to your brother
you should blithely
on the inheritance and confidently;
it is not fitting
that you should with sword
demand treasure from Fafnir.

These things were said by Regin to Sigurd. One day, when he came to Regin's house, he was well greeted.

Regin said:
13 Come hither
descendent of Sigmund,
the bold in counsel warrior,
to our halls;
he has more spirit
than an older man,
and I expect a fight
from a ravenous wolf.

14 I will feed
the troop-bold prince;
now has Yngvi's descendent
come to us;
this prince will be
mightiest under the sun,
over all the lands spreads
the *ørlög*-web.

Sigurd was always with Regin then, and he said to Sigurd that Fafnir lay in Gnitaheid and was in an worm's likeness; he possessed the Aegishiálm, that which all quickened-beings are fearful of.

Regin made Sigurd a sword, which was called Gram. It was so sharp that he put it in the Rhine and placed a tuft of wool before it in the stream, and the tuft was cut asunder as water. This sword Sigurd cleaved Regin's anvil with.

After that Regin egged Sigurd to slay Fafnir. He said:

15 High would laugh
Hunding's sons,
they who Eylimi's
life denied,
if the prince was more
disposed to seek
red rings
than to avenge his father.

Hialprek the king gave Sigurd ship-troops to avenge his father. They were overtaken by a great storm and tacked before a certain headland. A man stood on the cliff and said:

16 Who rides the
horses of Raevil
so highly,
on the roaring sea?
Sail-steeds are
sweat-splattered,
the sea-steeds cannot
withstand the wind.

Regin answered:
17 Here is Sigurd and myself
in the sea-tree,
to us is given a wind
with bane to ourselves;
steep breaking waves fall
higher than the ship's prow-boards,
the roller-steeds stumble;
who asks of this?

18 Hnikar they call me,
Hugin was gladdened when the
young Volsung
had battle.
Now you may call
the old man on the cliff,
Feng or Fiolnir;
I want to travel.

They turned to the land, and the old man went on the ship and it became calm.

19 Tell me this, Hnikar,
all you know about two things,
omens of gods and men:
which are the best
if one should fight,
omens at the sword-swinging?

Hnikar said:
20 Many are good,

if men know them,
omens at the sword-swinging;
a trusty companion
I think is the dark
raven to the sword-tree.

21 This is another,
if you are coming outside
and are prepared for the road:
two you look upon
standing on the walkway
men eager for fame.

22 This is the third,
if you hear the howl
of a wolf under ash-limbs:
good luck is granted
for you with helmet-staves,
if your see them before you go.

23 No man should
face the way
of the late-shining
sister of the moon;
they have victory,
who know how to look,
bold in sword-play,
and deploy the army in a wedge.

24 That is great mischief,
if you bump your foot,
when going to the battle-storm:
deceitful *dísir*
stand on two sides of you
and want to see you sore.

25 Combed and washed
should every wise one be
and in the morning fully fed;
because unseen is
where one goes in the evening;
ill is the luck of the careless.

Sigurd had a great battle with Lyngvi, Hunding's son, and his brothers. There Lyngvi fell and the three brothers. After the battle Regin said:

26 Now is the bloody eagle
by a sharp sword in
Sigmund's bane
*ríst* on the back;
none is greater,
he reddened earth, than
the king's heir,
and Hugin gladdened.

# Fafnir's Tale

*Untitled*

Sigurd went home to Hialprek. Then Regin egged Sigurd to kill Fafnir. Sigurd and Regin went up on Gnitaheid and came upon Fafnir's tracks, when he slithered to the water. Then Sigurd made a great pit in the path, and Sigurd went into it. And as Fafnir slithered off of the gold, he blew venom, and it came down upon the head of Sigurd. But as Fafnir slithered over the pit, then Sigurd laid his sword into his heart. Fafnir shook himself, and struck out with head and tail. Sigurd leapt out of the pit, and they saw each other. Fafnir said:

1 **A** youth and a boy,
of whom are you, boy, born,
who is your man, boy?
As you in Fafnir redden
your glittering sword:
standing in my heart is a sword.

Sigurd concealed his name, because it was believed in olden times, that words of a fey man had great strength, if he cursed his enemy with a name. He said:

2 Noble creature I am called,
but I have gone
as a motherless boy;
I have no father,
as the sons of living creatures,
I always go alone.

3 Do you know, if you had no father,
as the sons of living creatures do,
of what wonder begat you?

4 My family
I say is unknown to you
and myself the same;
Sigurd I am called,
Sigmund my father is called,
I have killed you with weapons.

5 Who was your whetstone,
why were you sharpened,
to end my life?
Boy with shining eyes,
you had a bitter father,

inborn the course is shown.

6 My spirit whet my
fully-capable hands
and my sharp sword;
few are sharp,
they become afraid,
if they are cowards in childhood.

7 I know, if you were able to grow
by your friends' breasts,
to me you seem to fight wrathfully;
now you are a captive
and a prisoner-of-war,
it is said the bound always tremble.

8 You unbraid me now, Fafnir,
because I seem to be far
from my father;
I am not a captive
though I was a prisoner-of-war,
you'll find I've loosened my life.

9 Hateful words only
you reckon in everything,
but I say to you one truth:
the ringing gold
and red-glowing treasure,
to you the rings are bane.

10 Authority over treasure
shall every man have
always until his last-day,
because one journey
shall every man
travel to Hel hence.

11 The doom of Norns
you will have before the headland
and be a foolish ape;
in water you will drown
if in a wind you row:
all is dangerous to the fey.

12 Tell me, Fafnir,
since you are said to be wise
and to know many things:
who are those Norns,
who come to those in need
and choose mother from child?

13 Born-apart
I say the Norns are,
they are not the same family;
some are kin to Aesir,
some are kin to elves,
some are Dvalin's daughters.

14 Tell me this, Fafnir,
since you are said to be wise
and to know many things:
what is the dueling-island called,
where sword-liquid is blended,
Surt and Aesir together.

15 Oskopnir it is called,
and there shall all
gods play at spears;
Bilrost is broken,
as they fare away,
and horses swim in the large river.

16 The Aegishiálm
I wore among men's sons,
while I lay on the treasures;
alone the strongest
I thought I was of all,
I did not find many men.

17 The Aegishiálm
protects no one,
where the wrathful shall fight;
they find that,
who come among many,
that no one is the sharpest.

18 Venom I snorted,
as I lay in the inheritance
mighty of my father.

19 Glittering worm,
you made great hisses

and had a determined spirit;
more wrathful,
the sons of freeholders are,
when they have the helm.

20 I counsel you now, Sigurd,
and you take the counsel
and ride home hence;
the ringing gold
and red-glowing treasure,
to you the rings are bane.

21 Counsel you have advised,
but I will ride to the gold,
that lies on the heath;
and you, Fafnir, lay
in life-breaking,
there so Hel may have you!

22 Regin betrayed me,
he will betray you,
he will be the bane of us both;
his life lose
I think that Fafnir must,
you now have more *megin*.

Regin was missing while Sigurd killed
Fafnir, and came afterwards, as Sigurd
wiped blood off the sword.

Regin said:
23 Hail to you now, Sigurd!
You have won victory
and Fafnir is gone;
of those men
who tread the earth,
I say you were raised bravest.

24 That is uncertain to know
when all men come together,
the sons of the victory-gods,
who was raised the bravest;
many are so sharp,
whose sword has not torn
into another's breast.

25 You are now glad, Sigurd,
and fain of the gains,
as you dry Gram on the grass;
my brother
you have mortally wounded,
but I myself caused it.

26 You advised
that I should ride

82

hence to the holy mountain;
treasure and life
the shining worm would rule,
except you questioned my heart.

Then Regin went to Fafnir and cut the heart out of him with a sword, called Ridil, and then he drank blood out of the wound afterwards.

27 Now, you sit, Sigurd,
and I will go to sleep,
and hold Fafnir's heart in the fire!
The heart
I will eat
after drinking the blood.

Sigurd said:
28 Far away you went,
while I in Fafnir reddened
my keen sword;
my strength
I had against the worm's *megin*,
while you lay in the heather.

Regin said:
29 Long laying
in the heather you would let
the old Jotun,
if you did not enjoy the sword,
what I myself made,
and your keen sword.

Sigurd said:
30 Spirit is better,
than a sword's *megin*,
where the wrathful shall fight;
because a brave man
I saw courageously fight
with a dull sword to victory.

31 Courage is better
than cowardice,
to have in battle-play;
cheer is better,
than fear,
whatever comes to hand.

Sigurd took Fafnir's heart and roasted it on a twig. When he thought that it was fully roasted and froth sweat from the heart, then he took his finger and tested that the heart was fully roasted. He was burned, and brought the

finger to his mouth. But Fafnir's heart-blood came onto his tongue, and he understood fowl-speech. He heard the small birds clucking in the bushes.

The birds said:
32 There sits Sigurd,
blood splattered,
Fafnir's heart
roasting on a twig;
wise I think would be to me
the spiller of rings,
if he the life-morsel,
sparkling, ate.

33 There lies Regin,
talking to himself,
wanting to deceive the boy,
he that trusts him;
in wrath are
evil words put together,
the smith of evil wants
to avenge his brother.

34 A head shorter
let him the high sage send
to Hel hence!
All the gold
then he may alone rule,
the heap that lay under Fafnir.

35 Wiser I think,
if he had known,
the great love-counsel of
you sisters;
thought about himself
and gladdened Hugin;
I expect a wolf
when I see his ears.

36 Is not so wise
the battle-tree,
the army protector, as I
thought would be;
if he lets the brother
come away,
when he has of the other
drained life.

37 Much foolish,
if he then spares
the warrior-crushing fiend;
there is Regin lying
and plotting on him;
he does not know to notice such.

38 A head shorter
   let him then the rime-cold Jotun be
   and dwell away from the rings;
   then will treasure
   that Fafnir had ruled,
   be with a single ruler.

39 So mightily shaped is not
   Regin to be
   my death-word bearer;
   because both the brothers
   shall soon
   go to Hel hence.

Sigurd cut the head from Regin, and
then he ate Fafnir's heart and drank
the blood of them both, Regin and
Fafnir. Then Sigurd heard what the
small birds said:

40 Bind up, Sigurd,
   the red rings,
   it is not like a king
   to be afraid of much;
   I know one maid,
   much the fairest,
   gold-enriched,
   if you might get her.

41 Lays to Giuki's
   the green road,
   forward points what is shaped
   for the host-traveler;
   there the dear king has
   begat a daughter,
   then will you, Sigurd,
   become engaged.

42 A hall is on high
   Hindarfial,
   it is all around the outside
   surrounded by fire;
   the wise have made the hall
   out of the shining
   light of Ogn.

43 I know on a mountain
   the battle-maid sleeps,
   and plays over her,
   the linden's destruction;
   Ygg struck with a thorn:
   had once killed
   a man, flax-Gefion,
   but not whom he had wanted.

44 You may, boy, see
   the maid under the helm,
   who away from the battle
   of Vingskornir rode;
   may not Sigrdrifa's
   sleep be broken,
   by a relative of Skioldungs,
   unless the Norns shaped it.

Sigurd afterwards rode Fafnir's tracks
to his lair and found it open, and doors
of iron and doorframes of iron and all
the timbers of the house were sank
into the earth. There Sigurd found very
much gold and filled two chests. Then
he took the Aegishiálm and a golden
mail tunic and the sword Hrotti and
many dear things and loaded these
on Grani. But the horse would not go
forward until Sigurd climbed on his
back.

# Sɪɢʀᴅʀɪꜰᴀ's Ꞇᴀʟᴇ

## *Untitled*

Sigurd rode up to Hindarfial and headed south to France. On the mountain he saw a great light, just as if a fire was burning, and it shined to the heavens. And when he came to it, there stood a shield-castle and a banner up over it. Sigurd went into the shield-castle and saw that there lay someone and they slept with all war-weapons. He first took the helmet off their head. Then he saw that it was a woman. Her armor was held fast as if it was grown into her flesh. Then he *ríst* with Gram from the head-opening of the armor downward, and so out along both arms. Then he took the armor off her, and she awakened and she sat up and saw Sigurd and spoke:

1 What pierced the armor,
what shook off my sleep?
Who from me fell
the pale constraints?
He answered:
Sigmund's son,
a short time ago tore
the raven's corpse-flesh
Sigurd's sword.

2 Long I slept,
long I was dreaming,
long are people's misfortunes;
Odin caused it,
so that I may not
break the sleeping-staves.

Sigurd sat down and asked her name. She then took a horn, full of mead, and gave him a memory-drink.

3 Hail Dag,
hail Dag's sons,
hail Nott and her kinswomen!
Eyes free of wrath
look on our meeting,
and give victory to the sitting one!

4 Hail Aesir,
hail Asynior,
hail to the beneficial earth!
Eloquence and intelligence
give to us two famous ones
and healing-hands while we live!

She was named Sigrdrifa and was a valkyrie. She said that two kings had fought; one was called Hialm-Gunnar, he was old and a great warrior, and Odin had named him victorious; but...

"...the other was called Agnar,
Auda's brother,
whom no wight
wanted to take."

Sigrdrifa killed Hialm-Gunnar in battle. And Odin stuck her with a sleep-thorn to repay this and said she would never afterwards have victory in battle and said she would be given in marriage.
"But I said to him, that I made strong oaths in this matter to be given to no man who was acquainted with fear." He spoke and asked her to teach him wisdom, if she knew tidings from all the worlds.

Sigrdrifa said:
5 Beer I give to you,
armor-Thing apple-tree,
blended with *megin*
and glory-*megin*;
it is full of songs
and help-runes,
good *galdr*
and game-runes.

6 Victory-runes you should *ríst*,
if you want to have victory,
and *ríst* on the sword-hilt,
some on the top-ring,
some on the handle-plate,
and name Tyr twice.

7 Ale-runes you should know,
if you want another's wife
to keep your troth, if you trust her;
on a horn they should be *ríst*
and on the back of the hand
and mark your nail with *Naud*.

8 The full cup shall be signed over
and against danger so protected
and throw a leek in the liquid:
I know this
that there will never be
mead harm-blended.

9 Help-runes you should know,
if you want help
and to loosen children from women;
they shall be *ríst* on the palms
and clasp the limbs
and ask the *dísir* to help.

10 Surf-runes you should *ríst*,
if you want to have safety
for the swimming sail-steeds;
on the stems they should be *ríst*
and on the rudder blade
and laid with fire in the oar;
the breakers aren't so steep
nor the blue waves,
you will come whole from the sea.

11 Limb-runes you should know,
if you want to be a leech
and know to see sores;
on bark they should be *ríst*
and on the tree's wood,
those whose limbs bow to the east.

12 Speech-runes you should know,
if you want no man to
repay hate with harm;
they are woven about,
they are all set together,
at the Thing,
where people should
go to full courts.

13 Spirit-runes you should know,

if you want to be of every
man strongest-willed;
they are read,
they are *ríst*,
they that Hropt considered,
from the liquid,
that had leaked
out of Heiddraupnir's skull
and out of Hoddrofnir's horn.

14 Stood on the rock
with Brimir's edge,
had on his head a helmet.
when Mim's head spoke
wisely the first word,
and said the true staves.

15 On the shield they are *ríst*,
the one before the shining god,
on Arvak's ear
and on Alsvinn's hoof,
on that wheel, that turns
under Rungnir's wagon,
on Sleipnir's tooth
and on the sled's fetters;

16 on the bear's paw,
and on Bragi's tongue,
on the wolf's claw
and on the eagle's nose,
on bloody wings
and on the bridge's tail,
on loosening palms
and on the helpful's footprint;

17 on glass and on gold
and on men's amulets,
in wine and malt
and on the wish-seat,
on Gungnir's point
and on Grani's breast,
on the Norn's nail
and on the owl's nose.

18 All were scraped off,
those which were *ríst*,
and stirred with the holy mead,
and sent on wide ways.
they are with the Aesir,
they are with the elves,
some are with the wise Vanir,
some the human beings have.

19 They are book-runes,
they are helpful-runes,
and all the ale-runes,
and mighty *megin*-runes,

whoever may unconfused
and unspoiled
have the good amulets,
enjoy them, if you take them,
until the Powers are rent.

20 Now you should choose,
since the choice is offered,
sharp weapon-maple;
speech or silence
to have for yourself in your spirit.
All harms are measured out.

21 I will not flee,
though I know I am fey,
I am not born of softness;
your loving-counsel
I want to have all of,
so long as I live.

22 This I advise you first,
that you with your kin
be flawless;
have no vengeance,
though they quarrel,
that is said to help the dead.

23 This I advise you second,
that you swear no oath,
unless in sincerity;
grim ties
go to the troth-breaker,
wretched is the vow-wolf.

24 This I advise you third,
if you are at the Thing
do not duel with the foolish man;
because the foolish man
often lets himself say
worse words than he knows.

25 All is in want

if you are silent;
you'll be thought a born coward,
or it is truly said;
dangerous is fool-talk,
unless you get good.
Another day
release his soul
and repay the lies among people.

26 This I advise you fourth,
if an evildoer lives,
full of vice, on the way:
going on is better,
than stopping to be a guest,
though night overtakes you.

27 Foresight-eyes
the sons of man need,
where the wrathful battle;
often bale-wise women
sit near the road,
they who dull swords and minds.

28 This I advise you fifth,
though you see fair
maidens on the benches:
silver-bought lovers
do not let them rule your sleep,
do not be seduced to kiss the girls!

29 This I advise you sixth,
though among men

[The Codex Regius is missing an
unknown number of pages at this
point; the missing section is called the
Great Lacuna. Where the text returns
after the Great Lacuna is an unknown
number of stanzas into another poem
about Sigurd. Because the title of the
next poem is missing, it is called, *A
fragment of a poem about Sigurd*.]

# A Fragment of a Poem About Sigurd

*Untitled*

quarrel done,
that you want the brave one
deprived of life?

2 To me has Sigurd
delivered oaths,
oaths delivered,
all lies;
thus deceived me,
when it should be
of all oaths
one that is completely trusted.

3 Brynhild has for you
prepared misfortune
inciting hatred,
to do harm;
she begrudges Gudrun
a good marriage,
and therefore you
she has to enjoy.

4 Some roasted wolf,
some worm cut into pieces,
some to Guthorm
given a share,
before they may,
desiring to harm,
on the wise man
lay hands on.

5 Sigurd was dead
on the south side of the Rhine,
a raven in a tree called loudly:
Atli will in you
redden edges,
battle-terrible ones will
be dropped by your oaths.

6 Gudrun stood outside,
Giuki's daughter,
and these words she
said first of all:

Now where is Sigurd,
leader of men,
my kinsmen are
riding ahead?

7 Only Hogni
gave an answer:
Sigurd has been split
by a sword's chop,
the gray horse droops its head
over the dead prince.

8 Then Brynhild said this,
Budli's daughter:
Well should you enjoy
weapons and land;
only Sigurd would have
ruled all,
if he a little longer
held onto life.

9 That did not seem right,
that he so ruled
Giuki's inheritance
and the Goths,
when he five sons
to command the host,
battle eager,
had gotten.

10 Then Brynhild laughed
—the entire hall resounded—
one time
with all her spirit:
Long should you enjoy
lands and subjects,
you who bold prince
let fall.

11 Then Gudrun said this,
Giuki's daughter:
You have said much
very atrocious;

evil ones may have Gunnar,
the slayer of Sigurd;
the hate-eager spirit
shall be avenged.

12 The evening was advanced,
much was drank,
then was everything
pleasantly related;
all slept,
when they went to bed,
only Gunnar was awake
very long.

13 His foot began to move,
he began to say many things,
the army-destroyer
began to think,
what they in the tree
both said,
the raven and eagle,
as they rode home.

14 Brynhild awakened,
Budli's daughter,
Skioldungs woman,
a little before day:
Whet me or stop me
—the harm is brought about—
sorrows to say
or let it be so!

15 All were silent
with these words,
few of them understood
the woman's behavior,
as she wept
began to speak of,
that which laughing
she asked the men.

16 It seemed to me, Gunnar,
grim in sleep,
all was cold in the hall,
my bed was cold;
and you, prince, rode,
wanting for rejoicing,

fetters held you
inside a fiend's army.
So will all of you
descendents of Niflungs
go deprived of strength:
you are oath-breakers.

17 You did not remember, Gunnar,
that you did that,
into a footprint the blood of you
both ran;
now you have to him entirely
paid evil,
when he the foremost of you
wanted to be.

18 Then learned that,
when he had ridden,
the courageous one to me
to ask for me,
how the army-destroyer
had first
held oaths
with the young prince.

19 A wound-wand was laid,
braided with gold,
the very-dear king
between us;
the edges were in fire
prepared outside,
and drops of poison
colored the inside.

This poem told of Sigurd's death, and it says here that they killed him outside. But some say such that they killed him inside in his bed sleeping. But German men say that they killed him outside in the forest. And such is said in the ancient *Lay of Gudrun*, that Sigurd and Giuki's sons had rode to the Thing, then he was killed. But in one way all say that they broke his trust and attacked him lying down and unprepared.

# The First Lay of Gudrun

*Guðrúnarqviða*

Gudrun sat over the dead Sigurd. She did not grieve as other women, but she was ready to burst from sorrow. Went both women and men to comfort her; but that was not easily done. Men say that Gudrun had eaten of Fafnir's heart and she understood fowl speech. This is also said about Gudrun:

1 Long ago, Gudrun
prepared to die,
as she sat full of sorrow
over Sigurd;
she did not wail
nor beat hands,
nor lament over it
like other women.

2 The jarls went,
very wise, forward,
they the hardened spirit
of her relieved;
yet Gudrun
could not grieve,
she was so moody,
she was nearly bursting.

3 Sat the glorious
brides of the jarls,
gold adorned,
before Gudrun;
each said their
own deep sorrow,
the most bitter that they
had suffered from.

4 Then said Giaflaug,
Giuki's sister:
I know in the world I am
the least desired,
I have five husbands
suffered loss,
two daughters,
three sisters,
eight brothers,
I alone live.

5 Yet Gudrun
could not grieve;
she was so moody
at the boy's death
and hard spirited
about the prince's corpse.

6 Then said this Herborg,
Hunaland's queen:
I have a harder
grief to say:
my seven sons
in the southern lands,
my husband the eighth,
fell on the battlefield;

7 father and mother,
four brothers,
on the rolling sea
the wind played,
the waves struck
against the ship's bulwark.

8 I myself should make stately,
I myself should prepare the burials,
I myself should handle
their Hel-journey;
all of that I suffered
in one season,
so to me no man
may seek after.

9 Then I was a captive
and prisoner-of-war
the same season
this happened;
I would dress
and bind the shoes

of the chieftain's wife
every morning.

10 She threatened me
because of jealousy,
and with hard
strikes drove me;
I found a house-master
never better,
and a house-mistress
never worse.

11 Yet Gudrun
could not grieve;
she was so moody
at the boy's death
and hard spirited
about the prince's corpse.

12 Then said this Gullrond,
Giuki's daughter:
You do not know, foster mother,
though you are wise,
the young wife
to talk to.
She advised against covering
the prince's corpse.

13 She jerked the coverlet
from Sigurd
and turned the pillow
before the wife's knees:
You look on the beloved,
press lips against the moustache,
as you once embraced
the healthy peacemaker.

14 Gudrun looked
one time,
she saw the prince's hair
running with blood,
the sparkling gaze
of the prince had passed,
the boar's spirit-fortress
cut by a sword.

15 Then Gudrun knelt
bent over the bolster;
loosened hair,
reddened cheeks,
and raining drops
ran down to her knees.

16 Then grieved Gudrun,
Giuki's daughter,

so that tears flew
into her tresses,
and yelled with
the geese in the courtyard,
the famous fowl
that the maid had.

17 Then said this,
Giuki's daughter:
Yours I know was
most loved
of all people
around the earth;
you wanted neither
outside nor inside,
my sister,
unless near Sigurd.

18 So was my Sigurd
near to Giuki's sons,
as a spear-leek
growing among grass
or as a bright stone
on a cord drawn,
a precious stone
over the nobles.

19 I thought myself and
the king's warriors
higher than everyone
of Herian's *dísir*;
now I am so little
as a leaf is
always in the bay-willow
at the boar's death.

20 I miss at the bench
and in the bed,
my conversation-friend,
Giuki's in-laws caused it;
Giuki's in-laws caused
my misfortune
and their sister's
sure grief.

21 So are the people
of the land devastated,
as you caused by
sworn oaths;
you will not, Gunnar,
enjoy the gold,
your arm-rings will
be a bane,
because you to Sigurd
swore oaths.

22 Often in the meadow
was more merriment,
before my Sigurd
saddled Grani,
and they to Brynhild
went to propose,
the wretched wight,
an ill omen.

23 Then said this Brynhild,
Budli's daughter:
Wanting is the wight
for husband and children,
whom you, Gudrun,
caused to grieve
and in the morning you
gave speech-runes.

24 Then said this Gullrond,
Giuki's daughter:
You be silent, hated one,
of these words!
The noble one's doom
you have always caused;
you drive every wave
ill shaped,
sorrowful sores
to seven kings,
and the ruin of friends
to most wives.

25 Then said this Brynhild,
Budli's daughter:

Atli alone caused
all this misfortune,
born to Budli,
my brother;

26 when in the hall
of the Hun people
fire on the boar's
serpent-bed shone,
I have for this trip
since paid,
they are ever since
seen by my eyes.

27 She stood near the place,
strength empowered,
burned Brynhild,
Budli's daughter,
fire came out of her eyes,
she breathed poison,
when she saw the sores
on Sigurd.

Gudrun went from there on the road to the forest of the wasteland and went all the way to Denmark and was there with Thora, Hakon's daughter, seven seasons.

Brynhild did not want to live after Sigurd. She caused to drop eight of her thralls and five house-servants. Then she laid on a sword until she died, as it is said in the *Short Lay of Sigurd*.

# A Short Lay of Sigurd

*Untitled*

1 It was long ago, that Sigurd
sought Giuki,
the young Volsung
had killed before;
took the troth
of the two brothers,
swore oaths
the strong-minded ones.

2 The maid was offered to him
and a multitude of treasures,
young Gudrun,
Giuki's daughter;
drank and conversed
many days together,
young Sigurd
and Giuki's sons.

3 Until they Brynhild
went to propose,
so with them Sigurd
rode as escort,
the young Volsung,
and knew the way;
he would have,
if he could have.

4 The southern man
laid a naked sword,
an inlaid sword,
in their middle;
not he the girl
tried to kiss,
nor the Hun king
lift into arms;
the very young maid
he intended for Giuki's son.

5 She herself a life
of shame did not know
and of appointed life
did not know harm,
neither a fault that is

nor is thought of.
In this went
the dire doom.

6 Alone she sat outside
in the day's evening,
until she so plainly
began to speak:
I shall have Sigurd
—or die!—
the very young man,
may be in my arms.

7 The words I now say,
I will rue after this,
Gudrun is his wife
and I am Gunnar's;
loathsome Norns
shaped our long sufferings.

8 Often she went out,
filled with evil,
on ice and glaciers,
every evening,
as he and Gudrun
went to bed
and Sigurd her
wrapped in cloth,
the Hun king
seduced his wife.

9 I have no hope of happiness
and husband both,
I will delight myself
with a grim spirit.

10 Began for her anger
to call for a slaughter:
You shall, Gunnar,
completely lose
my land
and me myself;
I will never be in love

with the prince.

11 I will go back
where I was before,
with close-born ones
my kinsmen;
there I will sit
and sleep away my life,
unless you Sigurd
let die
and other boars
are the best of.

12 Let the son go
as his father!
Should not raise the wolf
youngster for long;
for which the warrior's
vengeance becomes easier
to reconcile afterwards,
as the son lives.

13 Gunnar was wrathful
and downcast,
his spirit waivered,
sat around all day;
he knew what
he did not want to do,
what he was
befit to do,
or he was
best to do,
since he himself the Volsung
knew he would remove
and that Sigurd
is a great loss.

14 He had several thoughts
for a very long time;
that was not
customary in olden days,
for from the kingdom
a woman to go;
he began by getting Hogni's
oath of secrecy,
in him he had
complete trust.

15 To me only Brynhild
is best of all,
born of Budli,
she is the foremost of women;
first I should my
life lose,
rather than the maid

precious lose.

16 Will you for us the prince
deceive for treasure?
It is good to rule
Rhine metal
and be content
having treasure
and sitting
happily enjoying it.

17 Hogni one
answer granted:
It is not suitable for us
to do such,
sword rending
sworn oaths,
oaths sworn,
troth given.

18 We don't know on earth
men who are happier,
while we four
rule the people
and as the Hun
warlord lives,
not a greater
marriage on earth,
if we five sons
raise a long time,
for a good family
may produce.

19 I know completely,
whence the way stands:
Brynhild's passions
are too great.

20 We should Guthorm
egg for the killing,
the young brother,
untried;
he was outside when
oaths sworn,
oaths sworn,
troth given.

21 It was easy to egg
the not-eager-to-hesitate one,
stood in the heart
a sword in Sigurd.

22 Planned revenge
the battle-eager one in the hall
and hurled after

the one not-eager-to-hesitate;
to Guthorm flew
Gram with great force
wonderfully bright iron
from the king's hand.

23 His enemy fell
into two parts;
hands and head
of the enemy one way,
and the foot-part
fell away from the spot.

24 Sleeping was Gudrun
in bed,
sorrowless
near Sigurd;
but she awakened
far from joy,
when she knew Frey
was floating in blood.

25 She struck so hard
her hands,
that the spirit-strong one
rose up from the bed:
Do not grieve, Gudrun,
so bitterly,
very young bride,
your brothers live.

26 I have too young
beneficiary-heir,
he doesn't know to leave
from the enemy-home;
they have themselves
dark and dire
decided upon a
new plan.

27 There will not ride afterwards,
though there are seven,
sister's sons
such a one to the Thing;
I know completely
why this now goes:
only Brynhild wanted
all this misfortune.

28 Me the maid loves
before every man,
but with Gunnar
I did not do harm;
I did not violate relations,
sworn oaths,

lest I am not called
his wife's love.

29 The woman gave a sigh,
and the king his life,
she struck so hard
her hands,
that responded with her
the goblet in the corner
and yelled with her
the geese in the meadow.

30 Then laughed Brynhild,
Budli's daughter,
one time
with all her spirit,
when she in bed
could hear
the loud grief of
Giuki's daughter.

31 To her then said Gunnar,
the mercenary-prince:
You do not laugh at this,
woman eager-to-hate,
gladly on the floor,
because of good thoughts.
Why have you no
white appearance,
fomenter of evil?
I think, that fey you are.

32 You caused this
to happen woman,
that before our eyes
Atli was slain,
to see your brother's
bloody sores,
bleeding wounds,
you might bind over.

33 Men will not question you, Gunnar,
you have fought enough,
Atli will little notice
your enmity;
he will of you two
keep his soul longest
and always bear
more strength.

34 I will say to you, Gunnar,
—you know it yourself—
how you quickly
acquire reproach;
I was not too young,

nor too mature,
fully endowed with treasure
in my brother's hall.

35 Nor did I want that,
to have a husband,
before you Giukungs
rode into the courtyard,
three on horses,
the people's-kings,
but their journey
did not need to be done.

36 And this to me Atli
alone said:
to neither allow
division of the property,
gold nor land,
unless I let myself be given,
and no part
of the granted treasure,
that which to me
had been presented,
and a younger me
counted pieces of silver.

37 Then was doubt
in my spirit about this,
whether I should fight
or drop corpses in battle,
boldly, in armor,
contending against my brother.
That would then be known
by the people's-kings,
many men
would be grievous.

38 I let sink
our settlement;
I was overcome by desire
to get treasure,
red rings,
from Sigmund's son,
I did not of another
want wealth.

39 Then I promised myself to him,
who sat with gold
on Grani's back;
his eyes were not
like yours,
nor was any part
of his appearance;
though you thought you were
the people's-kings.

40 I loved one,
not several;
to bother with so much was not
in the spirit of the necklace-Skogul;
all this will Atli
find out afterwards,
when he asks of
the murder-journey I'll do.

41 That never should
a thin-minded woman
another's husband
accompany in life;
then will be vengeance
for my harms.

42 Up rose Gunnar,
prince of the retinue,
and on the woman's neck
laid his hands;
all went,
and several times,
of hale spirit,
to restrain her.

43 Pushed off her neck
each from herself,
let no man dissuade her
the long journey.

44 Then he with Hogni
urged secrecy:
I want all the men
to go in the hall,
yours with mine
—now there is great need—
to think about dissuading
the murder-journey of the woman,
before in time
harm comes;
then let us
decided what is needed.

45 Only this did Hogni
give in answer:
Don't let any man restrain
the long journey,
then her rebirth
will never again be!
Cranky she came from
her mother's knee,
she was always born
to be joyless,
many men
to sadden.

46 He turned downcast
from the conversation,
to where the land-of-jewels
dealt out treasure.

47 She searched through all
her possessions,
her bondwomen were dead
and the hall-women;
donned the golden mail tunic
—no good was in her heart—
before she pierced her body
on the edge of a sword.

48 Sank onto the pillow
she went further on,
and sword-wounded
thought what to say.

49 Now should go,
they who want gold
and less than that
think of me;
I gave everyone
an embellished pendant,
book and bedcover,
bright weeds.

50 All were silent,
thinking what to say,
and all at once
gave an answer:
Sufficient have died,
we want to live,
the hall-women have become
honored by deeds.

51 After careful consideration
the linen-adorned woman,
young of life,
spoke with these words:
I do not want anyone reluctant
nor difficult to persuade
for our sake
to lose life.

52 Though bones will
of yours burn
with less treasure,
when you come around,
—none of Menia's goods—
to visit me.

53 You sit down, Gunnar!
I will say to you,

life is without hope for
the bright bride;
your ship will not
leave the sound,
though I have
lost my soul.

54 You and Gudrun will reconcile,
sooner, than you think,
the wise woman has
with the king
sorrowful memories
of a dead husband.

55 There is a maid born,
mother raised;
who will be whiter
than the brightest day,
Svanhild, to be,
a ray of sunlight.

56 You will give Gudrun
to a certain good man,
to a destructive arrow
of many warriors;
will not be wanted,
not given happily,
her Atli is
going to have,
born to Budli,
my brother.

57 Many things I remember,
who opposed me,
they who to me bitterly
had betrayed;
joyless
during my life.

58 You will Oddrun
want to have,
but Atli will you
not let;
you will bow
secretly together,
she will love you,
as I should have,
if for us good was shaped
to happen.

59 You will Atli
persecute evilly,
you will be in a narrow
worm-pit laid.

60 And it will be

97

not much longer,
that Atli will
lose his soul
his happiness
and sons' lives.
Because Gudrun their
bed will smear,
sharp edges
from a sore heart.

61 It is fitting that Gudrun,
our sister,
her first husband
accompany in death,
if she was given
good advice,
or she had a spirit
like ours.

62 Not fast I now speak,
but she never will
for our sake
lose life;
she will be carried
on high waves
to Jonak's
ancestral land.

63 . . .
. . .
with care
Jonak's sons;
she will Svanhild
send from the land,
her daughter
and Sigurd's.

64 She will be bitterly
advised by Bikki,
because Jormunrekk
lives to destroy;
then will all perish
of Sigurd's kinsmen,
so is Gudrun's
grief increased.

65 I will ask you
one boon,
it will in this world
be the last boon:
let be prepared
a burial in the field,
put under us all
equal spaces,

they who died
with Sigurd.

66 Then cover the pyre
with tapestries and shields,
Welsh-cloth well colored,
and many Valir;
burn with me the Hun
on the other side.

67 Burn on the Hun's
other side
my servants,
adorned with necklaces,
two at the head,
and two hawks;
then all will be shaped
to the proper proportion.

68 Lay in the middle of us
metal ring-adorned,
sharp-edged iron,
as it laid once,
when we both
went to one bed
and were then called
a couple.

69 The jangle won't be
silent at his heel
at the door of the shining hall,
ring decorated,
if he accompanies
me on the journey hence;
our journey will not
be pitiful.

70 Because he goes with
five handmaidens,
eight servants,
a good lineage,
the slaves who grew up with me
and my patrimony,
that Budli gave to
his child.

71 Much I said,
I would more,
if to me more was measured
for speaking-time;
voice is dwindling,
wounds swelling,
I spoke truly,
so I will die.

# Brynhild's Ride on the Hel-way

*Untitled*

After the death of Brynhild, two pyres were prepared. One was Sigurd's, and it was burned first; then Brynhild was burned on the other. She was in a wagon, one with costly tapestries. So it is said that Brynhild went with the wagon on the Hel-way, and went past a homestead, where a certain *gýgr* lived. The *gýgr* said:

1 You shall through
not travel
the stone homestead
of my place;
it would seem better for you
to stretch tapestries,
rather than visit
another's husband.

2 Whom shall you visit
from Valland,
fickle-headed,
in my house?
You have, Var of gold,
if you desire to know,
compassionate one, hands,
washed in a man's blood.

3 Do not accuse me,
woman, from the stones,
though I went
on Viking expeditions;
I will of us
be thought nobler,
when men lineages
of ours remember.

4 You were, Brynhild,
Budli's daughter,
the unluckiest
born in the world;
you have Giuki's
children ruined
and their homes
destroyed the good.

5 I will tell you,
wisely, from the wagon,
very witless one,

if you desire to know,
how treated me
Giuki's heirs
loveless
and oath-breaking.

6 Let the form-shapers
the spirit-full king,
of eight sisters,
under an oak be;
I was twelve winters,
if you desire to know,
when to me the young prince
delivered oaths.

7 All called me
in Hlymdalir
Hild-under-the-helm,
everyone who knew me.

8 Then I let the old one
of the Goths
Hialm-Gunnar immediately
go to Hel;
I gave the younger victory
Auda's brother;
then Odin was with me
very angry about it.

9 He enclosed me in shields
at Skatalund,
red and white,
touching shields;
then he ordered to break
my sleep,
who of every land
knew no fear.

10 Placed around my hall

99

in the south,
the high burner
of wood;
then he ordered one warrior
to ride over,
the one who brought the gold
that laid under Fafnir.

11 The good one rode Grani,
the gold-distributor,
where my foster father
steered households;
only he was thought
better than all,
the Danish Viking
in the retinue.

12 We slept and stayed
in one bed,
as if he my brother
was born to be;
did not place

hands over the other
eight nights
laying together.

13 Yet accused me Gudrun,
Giuki's daughter,
that I Sigurd
had slept in the arms;
then I discovered,
what I did not want,
that they deceived me
in husband-taking.

14 Will be with too much sorrow
all too long
men and women
as they live;
we shall
never part,
Sigurd, together—
you sink, *gýgr*!

# Death of the Niflungs

*Dráp Niflunga*

Gunnar and Hogni then took all the gold, Fafnir's inheritance. A feud was then between the Giukungs and Atli. He blamed the Giukungs for the responsibility of Brynhild's loss-of-breath. Peace for this was made, that they should give him Gudrun in marriage, and give her a potion of forgetfulness to drink before she consented to be given to Atli. Atli's sons were Erp and Eitil. But Svanhild was Sigurd's daughter and Gudrun's.

Atli the king invited to his home Gunnar and Hogni and sent Vingi and Knefrod. Gudrun knew the treachery and sent along runes in words, stating that they should not come, and for a token she sent Hogni a ring, Andvari's Gift, and knotted on it a wolf's hair.

Gunnar had asked for Oddrun, Atli's sister, and did not get her; then he took Glaumvor, and Hogni had Kostbera. Their sons were Solar and Snaevar and Giuki—and when the Giukungs came to Atli, then bid Gudrun her sons, to ask for the Giukungs's lives. But they would not. The heart was cut out of Hogni, and Gunnar was set in a worm-pit. He struck a harp and put the serpents to sleep, but an adder stung him in the liver.

# The Second Lay of Gudrun

*Guðrúnarqviða*

Thiodrek the king was with Atli and had lost nearly all of his men. Thiodrek
and Gudrun lamented their woes between them. She spoke to him and said:

1 A maiden I was of maidens,
my mother nurtured me,
bright, in the bower,
I loved my brothers well;
until to me Giuki
delighted with gold,
delighted with gold,
gave me to Sigurd.

2 So was Sigurd
among Giuki's sons,
as a green leek
growing among grass,
or a high-boned hart
among fallow deer,
or gold glowing red
among gray silver.

3 Until begrudged to me
my brothers,
that I should have
the foremost of all;
sleep they could not have
nor the settling of disputes,
until they Sigurd
had killed.

4 Grani ran to the Thing,
the din was heard,
but then Sigurd
himself did not come;
all the saddle-beasts were
dripping sweat,
and as accustomed to toil
under the warriors.

5 I went grieving
to counsel with Grani,
wet-cheeked,
from the horse I sought tidings;

dropped Grani then
his head in the grass,
the horse knew that
his owner was not living.

6 Long I wavered,
long my thoughts were divided,
until I asked
the troop-ward about the prince.

7 Gunnar hung his head,
Hogni spoke to me
about Sigurd's
sore death:
Lies struck down
on the other side of the water
Guthorm's bane,
given to the wolves.

8 You can look for Sigurd
on the southern-way!
There you will hear
ravens yell,
eagles yell,
happy of food,
wolves howl
over your husband!

9 How can you to me, Hogni,
such a woeful thing,
without joy,
want to say this?
Your heart should be
torn by ravens
over the wide lands,
you know this.

10 Hogni answered
one time,
reluctant to have a good heart,

102

from great grief:
From this you will have, Gudrun,
more grief,
if my heart
ravens tear.

11 I turned away then,
from the conversation,
to the woods, to gather
the wolves' leavings;
I could not wail
nor slap hands,
nor lament over it
as other women,
there I sat dead
over Sigurd.

12 The night seemed to me
pitch-black darkness,
as I sat sorrowfully
over Sigurd;
the wolves seemed to me
better than all,
if they would lift from me,
loosen my life,
or burn me
as birch wood.

13 I journeyed from the mountain
five days all together,
until I the hall of Half,
high, recognized.

14 I sat with Thora
seven seasons,
the daughter of Hakon,
in Denmark;
she delighted me
with gold embroidered
southern halls
and Danish swans.

15 We had scripts,
that were warriors playing,
and on the handiwork
rulers of thanes,
red rounds,
Hun warriors,
sword-host, helm-host,
the king's company.

16 Sigmund's ships
glided from the land,
gilded figureheads,
carved stems;

we embroidered on the border,
that they fought,
Sigar and Siggeir,
south in Fivi.

17 Then heard Grimhild,
the Goth's queen,
what was in my heart;
she threw down the border
and summoned home her sons,
insistently,
asked about this,
which son would
compensate to the sister,
or the slain husband
would repay.

18 Gunnar prepared
gold to offer,
to compensate for the quarrel,
and Hogni the same;
she asked about this,
who would journey
to saddle a horse,
harness to wagons,
ride horses,
fly hawks,
shoot arrows
from yew-bows.

19 Valdar the Dane
with Jarizleif,
Eymod third
with Jarizkar;
they went in,
like boars
Langbard's troop,
had red cloaks,
magnificent mail tunics,
steep helms,
girded short swords,
had dark-brown hair.

20 To me each wished
to choose treasures
to choose treasures
and speak pleasantly,
as if they may from me
many sorrows
attain trust,
not could I prepare to trust.

21 Grimhild brought to me
a full cup to drink,
cool and bitter,

so I could not remember;
fortified with
dire *megin*,
the ice-cold sea
and blood of a sacrificial boar.

22 On the horn was
every kind of staff,
*ríst* and reddened
—I could not understand—
a long ling-fish,
Haddingiar's land
grain-ear uncut,
jaws of deer.

23 The beer was
many bales mixed together,
roots of all woods
and burned acorns,
the hearth-surrounding dew,
entrails from sacrifices,
swine liver broth,
because she was soothing hostilities.

24 And then forgot,
what had been said,
all the boars
fallen to earth in the hall;
kings came
before my knee thrice,
before she herself to me
came to speak.

25 I give you, Gudrun,
gold as a gift,
very much treasure,
from your dead father,
red rings,
Hlodver's hall,
all the bed-curtains,
for the fallen boar.

26 Hun maids,
they who tablet-weave
and prepare fair gold,
so that you can take delight,
alone you shall control
Budli's riches,
adorned with gold
and given to Atli.

27 I will not
go with the husband
nor Brynhild's
brother have,

it is not proper to me,
with Budli's sons
to increase family
nor to love life.

28 Do not be concerned with men's
hateful deed repayment,
what we have
caused to happen before;
thus you shall be
as if the both lived,
Sigurd and Sigmund,
if you nurtured sons.

29 I may not, Grimhild,
go forth rejoicing
nor battle-ready one
be hopeful for,
since Sigurd
sorrowfully drank
the carrion-monster, Hugin
the heart-blood together.

30 Then have I of all
noble lineage
found the prince,
and foremost superior;
he you shall have,
until your life is toppled,
be husband-less,
unless you take this one.

31 Stop trying to offer
balefully,
insistently,
this kin to me!
He will for Gunnar
do harm
and from Hogni
cut the heart.
I will not restrain,
until the energy-full
edge-player, incite
to take his life.

32 Grieving Grimhild
grasped the words
that her sons
would get misfortune
and her boys
mighty outrages.

33 Land I give to you,
an escort troop,
Vinbiorg, Valbiorg,

if you want these;
you will have them all your life
and love it, daughter!

34 Then will I choose
from the kings,
and only because kinsmen
have coerced me;
won't be to me
a husband to love,
nor will a brother's bale
shelter boys.

35 At once was on horse
every warrior seen,
and Welsh wives
heaved up into wagons;
seven days we
rode cold lands,
and another seven
beat waves.
And the third seven
climbed dry land.

36 There gate-keepers
at the high fortress
opened the gates,
before we rode into the courtyard.

37 Atli awakened me,
thought that I was
full of evil disposition
at the death of kinsmen.

38 So just now me
the Norns awakened,
troublesome portents
that I could interpret;
I thought you, Gudrun,
Giuki's daughter,
a sword blended with malice
laid through me.

39 That is for fire,
to dream of iron,
for self-deception and desires

is women's wrath;
I will with your injuries
bring fire,
to take care of you and leeches,
though to me it is loathsome.

40 I thought here in the courtyard
twigs fell,
those whom I wanted
to let grow,
cracked at the roots,
reddened in blood,
carried to the bench,
offered to me to chew.

41 I thought from my hand
hawks flew,
meat-less,
to a house-of-misfortune;
their hearts I thought
I ate with honey,
a troubled mind,
swelled with blood.

42 I thought from my hand
whelps loosed,
barking for lack of food,
both yelping;
their flesh I thought
to be like carrion,
corpses under duress
I should consume.

43 That speaks of
the discussion of slaughter
and the whiting
deprived of heads;
they will be fey
in a few nights
a little before daybreak
eaten by the troops.

44 Laid I afterwards
—I wanted no sleep—
defiant in the sick-bed;
that I do remember.

# The Third Lay of Gudrun

*Qviða Guðrúnar*

Herkia was the name of Atli's bondmaid; she had been his lover. She said to Atli, that she had seen Thiodrek and Gudrun both together. Atli was then very unhappy. Then Gudrun said:

1 **W**hat is it, Atli?
Always, Budli's son,
you are sad in spirit;
why do you never laugh?
It would be better
thought by the jarls,
if you spoke with the people
and looked upon me.

2 This grieves me, Gudrun,
Giuki's daughter:
to me in the hall
Herkia said,
that you and Thiodrek
under one roof slept
and lightly
in the linens were.

3 I will to you all this
make oaths on,
on the white
holy stone,
that with Thiodrek's son I
did not do anything,
a woman nor a man should not do.

4 Except I embraced
the war-leader,
the blameless boar,
one time;
the other was
our conversation,
when we two sorrowfully
inclined in secrecy.

5 Thiodrek came here
with three tens,
not one of them lives,
of three tens of men;

took away from me brothers
and ones dressed in armor,
took away from me all
next-of-kin.

6 Send for Saxi,
the southern prince!
He knows the holy
seething cauldron.

7 Seven hundred men
went into the hall,
before the king's woman
reached in the kettle.

8 Gunnar will not come now,
I did not call Hogni,
I will not see again
beloved brothers;
Hogni would with a sword
avenge such sorrow,
now I will myself have to
purge the crime.

9 She drew to the bottom
bright palms,
and she took up
precious stones:
See now, warriors
—I am acquitted,
the holy way—
see how the cauldron boils.

10 Laughed then Atli's
spirit in his breast,
when he saw whole
Gudrun's hands:
Now shall Herkia
go to the cauldron,

she who for Gudrun
intended harm.

11 The men watched wretchedly,
everyone that saw it,
how Herkia's
hands became singed;
they led the girl
to a foul mire,
so then Gudrun
repaid her misfortune.

# Oddrun's Lament

*Untitled*
*Titled derived from last line of stanza 33*

Heidrek was the name of the king, his daughter was called Borgny. Vilmund was the name of the person who was her lover. She could not beget children before came Oddrun, Atli's sister; she had been the love of Gunnar, Giuki's son. About this saga is here said.

1 I heard said
in ancient sagas
how a maid came
to Mornaland;
no one
on the earth
Heidrek's daughter
could help.

2 It was heard by Oddrun,
Atli's sister,
that the maid had a
great malady;
she brought from the stall
a steering-bit-equipped one,
and on the dark one
laid a saddle.

3 She let the mare travel
level earth-ways,
until it came to a high
standing hall,
and she went in along
the length of the hall;
she jerked the saddle
from the underfed horse,
and these words
she said first of all:

4 What is renowned
on the earth,
or what is famous
in Hunaland?
Here lies Borgny,
overcome with birth-labor,
your friend, Oddrun,
try, if you can help!

5 Which prince has
caused the disgrace?
Why is Borgny
suddenly ill?

6 Vilmund he is called,
the mercenary friend,
he wrapped the maid
in warm bedcovers,
five winters altogether,
so she hid it from her father.

7 Then I think was said
little more,
the compassionate one went and sat
at the knee of the maid;
mighty Oddrun yelled,
powerfully Oddrun yelled,
bitter *galdr*,
to Borgny.

8 A girl and a boy could
tread the earth,
blithe children
for Hogni's bane;
began to speak
the deathly-ill maid,
as she had not said
words before:

9 So help you
holy wights,
Frigg and Freyia
and more gods,
as you dropped from me
the danger.

10 I did not kneel
to help you,
as you were
never worthy;
I promised and I fulfilled,
when I said hither
so that I everyone
could help,
whoever the prince's
inheritance shares.

11 You are insane, Oddrun,
and out of your wits,
that you to me hostile
most words say;
because I accompanied you
on earth,
as if we of two brothers
were born.

12 I remember, what you said
one evening,
when I for Gunnar
prepared a drink;
such things you said would not
be done afterwards
by maids,
except to me alone.

13 Then took a seat
the troubled girl,
to tell misfortune
about her grief:
I was brought up
in the boar's hall
—most rejoiced—
to men's council.

14 I lived happily
and with my father's possessions,
five winters only,
while my father lived;
then spoke
his last words
the weary king
before he died.

15 To me he bid be endowed
with red gold
and given to the south
to the son of Grimhild;
and he to Brynhild
bid a helm be given,
he said she a wish-maid
would be.

16 He said the noblest
of all would be
the maid in the world,
unless the Measurer spoiled it;
and Gunnar
I got to love,
the arm-ring dealer,
as Brynhild should have.

17 Brynhild in the bower
stretched the border-cloth,
she had troops
and land of her own;
the earth shook
and the upper heavens,
when Fafnir's bane
recognized the fortress.

18 Then was war fought
with Welsh swords,
and the fortress broken,
the one Brynhild owned;
it was not long after this,
woefully rather shortly,
before their plans
were all known.

19 She caused the harsh
vengeance to happen,
that we all have
enough experienced;
it will to men
in every land be known,
that she let herself die
beside Sigurd.

20 They offered Atli
red arm-rings
and my brother
no small compensation;
offered to him for me
fifteen farmsteads,
Grani's side-load,
if he would have it.

21 But Atli said
he did not want it,
never would
from Giuki's sons;
we could not
resist with love,
so I held my head
against the ring-breaker.

22 Many spoke

109

of my kinsman,
said we had
been found together;
but Atli said I
would not
be guilty of an error
nor do any wrong.

23 But such should
never be denied by
a man before another,
when love is shared.

24 Atli sent
his messenger
through the Myrkvid,
to put me to the test;
and they came
where they should not come,
where we spread
one bedcover.

25 We offered the thanes
red arm-rings,
that they would not to
Atli say;
but they excitedly
spoke to Atli
and hastily
sped home.

26 And they to Gudrun
concealed it,
although she would
rather have known.

27 The roar was heard
of golden-hooves,
when into the court rode
Giuki's heirs;
from Hogni they
cut the heart,
and in the worm-pit
laid another.

28 I was journeying
one time
to Geirmund,

to prepare drinks;
the wise king
plucked a harp,
because he thought I
to help
the king of great lineage
would come.

29 I heard
from Hlesey,
how of strife
the strings spoke;
I bid the bondwoman
to be prepared.
I wanted the prince's
life to save.

30 We let float
over the sound,
until I saw all
Atli's courts.

31 Then came the wretched one
out quickly,
Atli's mother,
she should waste away!
And Gunnar's
heart was cut
so that I could not
save the famous one.

32 Often I wonder about it,
why I afterwards may,
the serpent-pillow Bil,
hold onto life,
when I the quick-to-battle one
thought I loved,
the sword dealer,
as myself.

33 You sat and listened
while I said to you
many evils that were shaped,
mine and theirs;
every man lives
as they choose—
now is passed
the lament of Oddrun.

# The Lay of Atli

*Atlaqviða in Grœnlenzca*
*Although stated as being "Greenlandic," the title is believed by scholars to be in error.*

Gudrun, Giuki's daughter, avenged her brothers, such is famously known: She first killed Atli's sons, and after killed Atli and burned the hall and all the retinue. About this is this poem composed.

1 Atli sent
a messenger to Gunnar,
the knowledgeable man rode,
Knefrod was his name;
he came to Giuki's courtyard
and to Gunnar's hall,
the benches around the hearth
and sweet beer.

2 The retainers drank there
—and the concealers were silent—
wine in the Welsh-hall,
they saw the Hun's wrath;
then Knefrod called
in a cold voice,
the southern man.
—he sat on the high bench:

3 Atli sent me here
riding with a message,
the mare bit-clamping,
in the unknown Myrkvid,
to bid you two, Gunnar,
to come to the bench
with helms around the hearth,
to visit Atli's home.

4 There you can choose shields
and shaved ash,
red-gold helms
and a host of Huns,
silver-gilt saddle-cloth,
blood-red shirts,
lances, darts,
bit-clamping steeds.

5 He will also give to you the vale
of the wide Gnitaheid,
screaming spears
and gilded ship-stems,
great treasures
and Danparstadir,
the forest that is famous,
that men call Myrkvid.

6 Then Gunnar turned his head
and said to Hogni:
How do you counsel us, young man,
since we hear such?
Gold I do not know
on Gnitaheid,
that we did not have
another just the same.

7 We have seven hall-houses,
full of swords,
every one of their
hilts of gold;
I know my mare is best,
and sword sharpest,
bow is bench-seemly,
and mail shirt made of gold,
helm and shield whitest,
to come out of Kiar's hall;
one of mine is better
than all of the Huns'.

8 What do you think the lady meant,
when she sent us the arm-ring,
wrapped in heath-dweller's weeds?
I think, that she bid warning;
I found a heath-dweller's hair
wound on the red ring:
wolfish is our way

111

to ride on this errand.

9 No kinsman whetted Gunnar
nor another neighbor,
confidant nor adviser,
nor any who are powerful;
said then Gunnar,
as a king should,
glorious, in the mead-house,
with great spirit:

10 Rise up now, Fiornir,
let along the benches wade
the brave men's golden cups
in men's hands!

11 The wolf will rule
Niflungs' inheritance,
old gray guardians,
if Gunnar is missed,
black-pelted bears
bite with fangs,
the bitch-stud rejoices
if Gunnar does not come back.

12 Led the land-ruler
the valiant troops,
weeping, battle-whetter,
the Huns from the court.
Then said this to the young
inheritance-guard of Hogni:
Hale journey now and wisely,
where your heart desires!

13 The brave ones led the steppers
at a run over the mountain,
the bit-champing mares,
in unknown Myrkvid;
all of Hunmork shuddered,
as the hard-hearted ones passed,
drove their switch-shy ones
through all-green valleys.

14 They saw Atli's land
and deeply guarded watchtowers,
Bikki's warriors standing
on the high fortress,
the hall over the southern-people,
surrounded by seat-trees,
bound rounds,
shining shields,
spears, darts,
and there Atli drank
wine in the Welsh-hall;
the guards sat outside,

they warded for Gunnar,
if they came here visiting
with screaming spears
to awaken the prince's war.

15 Their sister perceived first
as they came in the hall,
both her brothers,
beer had she little drank:
You are now betrayed, Gunnar,
what will, mighty one, help you
with the Hun's harmful schemes?
Quickly go out of the hall!

16 You would've been better, brother,
if you traveled in armor,
likewise in helms around the hearth,
to see Atli's home;
sat in a saddle
sun-bright days,
need-paled corpses,
let the Norns grieve,
Hunnish shield maidens
know the harrow,
and Atli himself
you could let be in the worm-pit;
now that worm-pit
is destined for you.

17 It is too late now, sister,
to gather Niflungs,
long will you search
for the troops of the Rhine
from the red-mountains,
the valiant warriors.

18 They seized Gunnar
and set in fetters,
the friend of Borgunds,
and bound his feet.

19 Hogni struck down seven
with a sharp sword,
and the eighth he thrust
in the hot fire;
so shall the brave
defend against fiends,
as Hogni warded
for Gunnar.

20 Asked the brave,
if for life would,
the Goths' prince
offer gold.

112

21 Hogni's heart shall to me
lay in hands,
bloody, from the breast
cut from the bold-rider,
a sharp biting sax,
the prince's son.

22 They cut the heart
out of Hialli's breast,
bleeding, and laid it on a platter
and brought it before Gunnar.

23 Then said this Gunnar,
leader of men:
Here I have the heart
of cowardly Hialli,
unlike the heart
of brave Hogni,
it trembles much
as it lies on the platter,
trembles half as much
as when it laid in his breast.

24 Hogni then laughed,
as the heart was cut
that quickened the helmet-smith,
since he didn't think to cry out;
bloody it was laid on a platter
and brought before Gunnar.

25 Said this Gunnar,
the spear-Niflungs:
Here I have the heart
of brave Hogni,
unlike the heart
of cowardly Hialli,
it trembles little,
as it lies on the plate,
trembled not so much
when it lay in his breast.

26 So you shall, Atli,
be far from eyes,
as the treasure
will be;
under me alone
all is concealed
the Niflungs hoard;
now Hogni is lifeless.

27 Always was in doubt to me
while we both lived,
now it is not to me,
as I alone live;
Rhine shall rule

the metal men quarreled over,
the Aesir-descended
inheritance of the Niflungs,
in surging waters
the Welsh arm-rings shine,
rather than gold on the hands
of Hun born shine.

28 Turn the wagon-wheels!
The captive is now in bonds!

29 Atli the powerful
rode Glaum's mane,
covered in battle-thorns,
their blood relation;
Gudrun the victory-god
guarded against tears,
destitute in the tumultuous hall.

30 So it goes for you, Atli,
as you had with Gunnar
often swore oaths
and long ago called,
on the sun in the southern-hall
and on Sigtyr's mountain,
the horse of the bed of rest,
and Ull's ring.

31 And afterwards
the bridled one drew
the treasure-guarding battle-ruler
to death's vessel.

32 The living prince
they laid in the yard,
that was crawling,
many men,
inside with worms;
and Gunnar alone,
wrathfully-minded, harp
struck with hands.
The strings thundered,
so shall the gold
ring-divider boldly
be protected while alive.

33 Atli led
toward his lands
the gravel-treading horse
away from the murder;
a din was in the courtyard,
a throng of horses,
men's weapon-songs,
had come from the heath.

34 Gudrun then went out,
to meet Atli,
with a gilded goblet,
to present repayment to the ruler:
You can receive, prince,
in your hall,
gladly from Gudrun
noise-makers gone to Niflhel.

35 Resounded the ale-cups
of Atli, heavy with wine,
when in the hall altogether
the Huns gathered,
men with long-moustaches,
each went in.

36 Quickly then the bright-faced one
brought them drinks,
the terrible *dís*, to the boars,
and brought ale-food,
repulsed, pale-faced,
and said offensive things to Atli.

37 You have your sons',
sword-dealer,
corpse-bloody hearts
chewed with honey;
you have digested, moody one,
man-flesh from the battlefield,
eating it as ale-food,
and sending it to the high-seat

38 You will never call after this
to your knee
Erp and Eitil,
two ale-cheerful ones;
you will not see after this
amidst the seats
gold distributors
making spears,
cutting manes
nor driving mares.

39 A din was on the benches,
a terrible song from the men,
a din under costly-woven cloth,
the Huns grieved,
except for Gudrun alone,
as she never grieved
for her bear-fierce brothers
and sweet sons,

young, untried,
whom she got with Atli.

40 Sowed gold
the gosling-bright one,
red-rings
she delighted the servants;
she let what was shaped grow,
and the shining metal go forth,
the woman did not
care about the living.

41 Unaware, Atli,
he had drunk himself weary,
he did not have a weapon,
he did not ward against Gudrun;
often their play was better,
when they would gently
embrace often
before the nobles.

42 She bid with a sharp tip,
gave blood to drink,
a hand eager-for-death,
and loosed the whelps;
pushed before the hall doors
and awakened the servants,
a fire-brand, the bride, hot,
thus she avenged her brothers.

43 Then she gave fire to all,
those that were inside
who from Granmar's murder
come out of Myrkheim;
the ancient timbers fell,
the temple smoked,
Budlungs's homestead
burned and shield-maidens
inside, life-stemmed,
sank in the hot fire.

44 Enough is said about this;
so has never since
a bride in armor
avenged her brothers;
she had three
people's-kings
become death-word,
the bright one, before she died.

But this is told in detail in the
*Greenlandic Lay of Atli.*

114

# Ⴅⱨℇ Ꮐⱃℇℇⴖⱡⱥⴖ◗ℐⲥ Ⱡⱥⲩ ⲟⴼ Ⱨⱦⱡℐ

*Atlamál in Grœnlenzco*

1 The old enmity was related,
when once in the courtyard
men met together,
that was useful to few;
a private conversation,
terrible were they afterwards,
and the same to Giuki's sons,
who were totally betrayed.

2 The Skioldungs' destiny grew
—should not have been fey—
Atli was ill advised,
though he had insight;
dropped strong supports,
greatly caused himself harm,
quickly sent an invitation
to his in-laws to come soon.

3 The house-lady was wise,
used her woman's intuition,
she heard the lay of the words,
what they spoke in secret;
next came a difficult idea,
she wanted to help them,
would sail over the sea,
but she herself could not go.

4 *Ríst* runes,
Vingi distorted them
—danger was he the promoter of—
before he handed them over;
then journeyed afterwards
Atli's messengers
over the Limafiord,
where the brave one lived.

5 Were very hospitable
and kindled a fire,
thought they were not deceitful,
those who had come;
took their gifts,
the women sent them
to be hung on the pillar,
did not think they were important.

6 Came then Kostbera,
she was Hogni's wife,
she had an observant nature,
she addressed them both;
was glad and was Glaumvor,
whom Gunnar had,
the wise didn't fail to serve-truly,
attended the guests' needs.

7 They bid Hogni to their home,
rather than ask if he would go;
their duplicity was shown,
if they had their guards;
then Gunnar agreed,
if Hogni wanted to;
Hogni thus did not refuse
as he had decided.

8 Maidens brought mead,
many were then passed,
many horns then passed,
until they were completely drunk;
the couple readied for rest,
when they thought it proper.

9 Learned was Kostbera,
she knew to distinguish runes,
to pronounce word-staves
in the firelight;
her tongue was guarded
bided in her gums:
they were so confused
that they were without meaning.

10 Went to bed afterwards
Hogni and she;
the hospitable one dreamed,
concealed nothing,
said to the wise king,
immediately when she awoke:

11 You prepare to leave home, Hogni,
consider advice!
Few can know about the runes,

you should go another time!
I read the runes,
that your sister *ríst*,
the bright one has not you
bid at this time.

12 The only thing I wonder about most
—I cannot understand it:
why the wise one
would *ríst* confusedly;
because it was indicated
that there was an undertone
of death to you both,
if you came at once;
the woman wants for a staff,
or another is responsible.

13 All are malevolent, said Hogni,
I do not have this habit,
I will not look for this,
unless I have to repay them;
the prince will us gold
delight glowing-red,
I am never afraid
though frightful things are known.

14 You will go to your downfall,
if you persist thence,
you will a welcome
not get this time.
My dreams, Hogni,
are not concealed:
you will go against-the-oars,
or else I am too fearful.

15 I thought your bedcover
burned with fire,
high flames spread
throughout my house.

16 Here lay linen-clothes,
they are of little value,
they will soon burn,
they are the bedcovers you saw.

17 A bear I thought came in here,
breaking up the bench-sticks,
shaking his paws so
that we were frightened;
had many of us in his mouth,
so that we were powerless;
that and the trampling
did not seem so minor.

18 A storm is growing,
it will soon be daybreak;

thinking of white-bears:
that would be an eastern storm.

19 An eagle I thought flew in here
all along the house,
that dealt very much to us,
splashed us all in blood;
I thought from its threats,
it had Atli's likeness.

20 We slaughter soon,
then we'll see blood;
often that is for oxen,
dreaming of eagles;
Atli's disposition is hale,
whatever is in your dreams.
Let that end,
every conversation passes.

21 The well-born awakened,
there was the same example,
Glaumvor was cautious,
there were harmful dreams;
about these Gunnar
found two ways.

22 Prepared I thought the gallows,
you were going to hang,
worms ate you,
I lost you while you were quick,
Ragnarok began;
counsel me, what that was!

23 Bloody I thought a sword
came out of your shirt,
evil is such a dream
to say to a relative;
a spear I thought stood
in the midst of you,
howling wolves
at both ends.

24 There are dogs running,
they bark very much,
often barking hounds are
for flying spears.

25 A river I thought ran in here
all along the house,
noisy in its fury,
surging from the benches;
broke both the feet
of the two brothers here,
the water would not retreat;
that should be for something.

116

26 I thought the dead women
came here in the night,
were scantily adorned,
wanting to choose you,
bid you at once
to their benches;
I say limbless
are your *dísir*.

27 It is too late to say,
it is now decided;
the danger cannot be avoided,
since we have decided to go,
many things indicate
that we will be short-lived.

28 The light of dawn was seen,
they were eager
to rise up,
though others dissuaded;
five went together,
there were more,
twice as many house-man-servants,
this was thought a bad idea.
Snaevar and Solar,
they were Hogni's sons,
Orkning the other was called,
who accompanied them;
blithe was the protector,
his wife's brother.

29 The fair-dressed ones went,
until the fjord separated them,
the shining one dissuaded,
nothing said held them.

30 Said these words Glaumvor,
whom Gunnar had,
she spoke with Vingi,
as she thought to:
I do not think the hospitality will be
as we want;
a crime is the coming of a guest
if it is so prepared.

31 Then Vingi swore,
he spared little in the decision:
May Jotuns have him,
if he lies to you,
the gallows are complete,
if he plots against safety.

32 Bera said these words,
blithe in her spirit:
Sail in good fortune,
and victory in your errand,

go, as I say so!
No one can deny this.

33 Hogni answered
—thought well of his kin:
You be content, wise ones,
however it goes!
Many say this,
thought it missed the mark,
many care little,
how they are escorted from home.

34 They watched afterwards,
before they separated:
I think the outcome was shaped,
when they parted ways.

35 The powerful began to row,
broke the keel in half,
rowed with falling backs,
became angry;
the oar-thongs tore,
the pins broke,
they did not secure the vessel,
before they turned away.

36 A little time later
—I will tell the end of this—
they saw the farmstead,
that Budli owned;
the gate creaked loudly,
as Hogni struck it.

37 Then Vingi said the words,
that were best unsaid:
Get away from the house!
It is dangerous to approach,
soon I will have you burned,
quickly shall we strike,
fair I bid you come,
though dangerous in undertone,
or bide here
while I build your gallows!

38 Hogni said these words
—pausing little to think—
wary not one whit,
as was found out later:
Do not seek to frighten us,
seldom put that forward!
If you increase your words,
it will increase your misfortune.

39 They fell upon Vingi
and dropped him to Hel,

laid with axes,
while his soul faded.

40 Atli gathered them together
and went in armor,
went so prepared,
into the palisade;
threw words
all at once became angry:
It was resolved before
to take away your life.

41 One can poorly see,
if it had been decided before,
because you are unprepared,
and one has fell,
lambasted to Hel,
one of your troop.

42 They were enraged,
when hearing these words,
moved their fingers
and clutched spear-straps,
shot sharply
and shields protected them.

43 Then came inside a report,
what was engaged outside,
loudly before the hall;
heard a thrall say it.

44 Enraged was Gudrun then,
as she heard the troubles,
laden with arm-rings,
she cast them off completely,
slung the silver so
that the rings broke asunder.

45 Afterwards she went out,
raised the doors,
did not go timidly,
and greeted with joy who had come;
turned to the Niflungs,
so was the last greeting,
completely sincere,
she said more:

46 I tried to help,
to restrain you at home,
what is shaped no man can stop,
and so shall you come here.
Spoke with all her mother-wit,
if they would be reconciled,
all said no.

47 Then saw the high-born ones,
as they played at wounds,
thought of harsh deeds
and threw off her cloak;
naked she took a sword
and guarded for her kinsmen,
was skillful at battle,
where she set her hands.

48 Giuki's daughter let
two young warriors fall,
she struck Atli's brother,
he was carried afterwards,
she shaped her fighting so,
slashed his feet from under him.

49 Another she decided to strike,
so that he could not rise up,
she had him in Hel;
her hands did not shake.

50 A battle then began,
that was widely extolled;
it surpassed all others,
the sons of Giuki did;
so is said of the Niflungs,
while they lived,
shaped the battle with swords,
slashed off armor,
hewed at helms,
as their spirits prevailed.

51 Fought most of the morning,
until the middle of the day passed,
all of daybreak
and the beginning of the day;
before there was enough fighting,
the vale flowed with blood;
eighteen, before falling,
they had bested,
Bera's two boys
and her brother.

52 The rash one began to speak,
though he was angry:
This looks very bad,
you caused this;
there were three tens,
formidable thanes,
afterwards eleven live,
our side will be burned.

53 There were four brothers,
then Budli was lost,

now Hel has half,
two lie dead.

54 I acquired mighty relations
—I cannot conceal this—
a baleful wife,
I had no advantage from this;
seldom had what I deserved,
since you happened to come to us,
took my kinsmen away,
often tricked me of treasure;
sent my sister to Hel,
such I feel the most.

55 Speak on this, Atli,
what you did before:
took my mother
and murdered for treasure,
wise daughter of mother's sister
you starved in a cave;
it seems laughable to me,
when you recount your injuries,
the gods I thank,
when you go badly.

56 I egg you on, jarls,
to increase the sorrows greatly
of the proud woman,
I want to see that;
try to strive
to make Gudrun yield!
That I may see
her with no happiness.

57 Take Hogni
and cut his flesh with a knife,
cut out his heart,
you should prepare for this;
grim-minded Gunnar
fasten on the gallows,
forge ahead to do this deed,
bid the worms come.

Hogni said:
58 Do it, as you wish!
I will wait gladly for this,
my rashness you will prove,
I have experienced steeper trials;
you had resistance,
while we were hale,
now we are hurt,
you may do as you want.

59 Beiti spoke
—he was Atli's steward:
We will take Hialli,

but spare Hogni!
We will finish half the task,
he is shaped-for-death,
however long he lives,
worthless he will always be called.

60 The cauldron-tender was terrified,
did not stay long at his post,
knew how to be timid,
climbed into every corner;
he said his lot was wretched,
that his labors should be so repaid,
and his day was dreary,
to die and leave the swine,
all the many things to chose from,
that he had before.

61 They took Budli's servant
and drew a knife,
the wretched thrall howled,
before feeling the point;
said they had him at their disposal,
to manure the field,
do the filthiest work,
if he could survive;
fain though he would be,
to have his life.

62 Hogni saw to this
—few would do so—
that the slave would get
to go away;
I say it is easier for me,
to carry out your sport,
why would we here want
to hear this screeching?

63 They seized the excellent one,
there was no possibility
the warriors of heroic stance
would deliberate and delay longer;
then Hogni laughed
the day laborers heard it,
he proved himself a champion,
he bore the torture well.

64 Gunnar took the harp,
moved it with sole-twigs;
struck it as he knew how,
to grieve the women;
the men lost spirit,
those who could hear it clearly;
he sang his condition powerfully,
the rafters burst asunder.

119

65 The precious one died then,
it was early in the day,
their death in the end
gave life to their prowess.

66 Mighty Atli thought to himself,
that he got them both,
told the misfortune to the wise one
and taunted her with the news:
It is now morning, Gudrun,
you are missing the loyal ones,
you yourself shaped it,
it has so gone.

67 You are fain, Atli,
you reveal your killings,
you will regret them,
if you find out everything;
afterwards will be a legacy
—I can say this:
misfortune you will never avoid,
unless I die, too.

68 I cannot deny such,
I see another course of action,
twice as fitting
—often good is rejected:
I will console you with girls,
splendid valuables,
snow-white silver,
as you yourself wish.

69 Is no hope for this,
I do not want these,
I break the agreed upon peace,
for smaller reasons;
terrible I was thought before,
I will now increase it,
I endured everything
while Hogni lived.

70 We were raised
in one house,
played many games
and grew in the grove,
Grimhild provided us
gold and neck-rings;
my brother's slaying will
never be compensated for,
nor will this ever
for me be considered.

71 Women's prospects drop
if men are tyrants,
to king falls to his knees

if the pawns dwindle,
the tree falls
if the roots are chopped underneath;
now only you may, Atli,
rule over all here.

72 He was very shallow minded
for the prince to believe this,
the duplicity seen,
if he had been on his guard.
Close was Gudrun then,
did not reveal her spirit,
she acted lightly,
she played with two shields.

73 She made much ale-drinking
to her brother's legacy,
and Atli said the same
is prepared for him.

74 They let this be concluded,
the drinks were prepared;
the gathering was
with very much destruction;
strong was her scheming-heart,
she harmed Budli's family,
she wanted her husband
to suffer terrible revenge.

75 She enticed the little ones
and set them on the bench-stick;
the fearful ones were grim
and did not weep,
went into their mother's embrace,
asked would happen next.

76 Do not ask after that!
I intend to destroy you both,
the desire has been with me long,
to remedy you of old age.
Sacrifice your children if you wish,
no one will prevent it,
wrath's rest will be short,
if you do this deed.

77 Then the fierce one destroyed
the brothers' childhoods,
dealt justly,
she cut both their necks.
But Atli asked about,
where were
his boys playing,
as he saw them nowhere.

78 I decided to go over

to say to Atli,
won't conceal it from you,
Grimhild's daughter;
no happiness will it be for you, Atli
if you find it out:
a great woe was awakened,
when you slew my brothers.

79 I have seldom slept much,
since they fell,
I promised you cruelty,
I will now remind you;
said to me it is morning,
I remember that,
and now it is evening,
you will hear such.

80 Your sons you have
lost, as you never should,
know that their skulls you
had as ale-cups.
I prepared your drinks:
their blood I blended in.

81 I took their hearts
and on a spit I roasted,
delivered to you afterwards,
said it was calf-meat;
you finished it alone,
you decided not to leave anything,
chewed greedily,
used your molars.

82 Now you know about your children
—few suffer worse—
I caused my actions
though it is not my boast.

83 You were grim, Gudrun,
that you could do so,
your children's blood
to blend in my drink;
you have wiped out your blood kin,
the least you should have done,
you allow me and yourself
little between misfortunes.

84 One wish I have is
to kill you yourself,
few are bad enough
to such a prince;
you have done before,
what is an example to men,
of folly, cruelty,
in this world;
now you have added one,

what is just now heard of,
grasped a mighty crime,
you've prepared your funeral feast.
85 You will burn on a pyre
but before be pelted with stones,
then you will have gained,
what you always demanded.
Say to yourself such
sorrows in the early morning!
I will have a fair death
fare to another light.

86 Sitting in the same house,
sending hostile thoughts,
catching words of hate,
neither one was content.
Wrathful grew the Hniflung,
thought of a great deed,
mentioned to Gudrun
that he was grim to Atli.

87 Came to her thoughts
Hogni's treatment,
told him it was good fortune
if he brought about revenge,
then Atli was killed,
bided a short time for this,
Hogni's son struck him
and Gudrun herself.

88 The rash one began to talk,
stretched out to sleep,
quickly realized he was dying,
of bandages he said he had no need:
Say this truthfully:
who killed Budli's son?
No little game was played with me,
I have no hope for life.

89 Conceal from you will not
Grimhild's daughter:
I caused this,
that your lifetime has passed,
and Hogni's son somewhat,
that your wounds exhaust you.

90 You have waded into strife,
though it was not fitting;
wrong is a friend's deceit,
they who trusted you well.

91 Reluctantly I left home,
to ask for you, Gudrun;
you were a praised widow,
causing ambitious things,

121

was no hope of a lie,
as we found out about;
you went home here,
a troop of men accompanied us,
all were noble
in our retinue.

92 Many were all our honors,
men of rank and dignity,
cattle were abundant,
made much use of them;
there was a multitude of treasure,
partaken by many.

93 I paid for the famous one,
gave many precious objects,
three tens of thralls,
seven good bondwomen;
such was becoming,
there was more silver though.

94 You say that all this seems
the same as if it were not,
while those lands lay,
that Budli left to me;
you dug from under us,
you got a portion.
You caused your mother-in-law
to often sit grieving,
I did not find a hale spirit
in our household afterwards.

95 Now you are lying, Atli,
though I little care;
rather I was seldom docile,
you brought it up very much;
the young brother quarreled,
brought strife in between,
half went to Hel
from your house;
everything faltered
that we should have profited from.

96 We were three siblings,
thought to be unyielding,
left from the land,
accompanied Sigurd;
sped quickly forward,
each steered a ship,
wandered as fate dictated,
until we came to the east.

97 A king was killed first,
chose land there,
held chieftains in our hands,
they showed fear;

fought out from the woods,
those we wanted to acquit,
set them in fortunes,
who had no possessions.

98 The Hun was dead,
then the prospects quickly dropped
strong was the young one's grief
had a widow's name;
the quick thought it was anguish
to come into Atli's household,
had a champion before,
it was a misfortunate loss.

99 You did not come from the Thing,
as we discovered,
that you sought a lawsuit
nor diminished another;
you wanted to always yield,
and never held fast,
you let it be calm
… … …

100 Now you are lying, Gudrun,
little will that better
either of our lots,
they have all been diminished;
now do this Gudrun,
from your goodness
to our honor,
as they carry me out.

101 A *knörr* I will acquire
and a stained coffin,
will well wax the cover
to be on your body,
think of every need,
as if we were loyal.

102 A corpse was then Atli,
caused kinsmen's pain to grow,
the high-born fulfilled
all that was promised;
wise Gudrun wanted
to take her own life,
the day was delayed,
she died another time.

103 Fortunate is everyone since,
who fathers such
well accomplished children,
as Giuki engendered;
will live on afterwards
in every land,
their words of defiance,
wherever people hear them.

# The Whetting of Gudrun

*Guðrúnarhvöt*

Gudrun went to the sea, when she had killed Atli, went out into the sea and wanted to end herself. She could not sink. She drifted over the fjord into the land of king Jonak. He took her.

Their sons were Sorli and Erp and Hamdir. There was raised up Svanhild, Sigurd's daughter. She was given to Jormunrekk the mighty. With him was Bikki. He counseled that Randver, the king's son, should take her. That was told to the king by Bikki. The king caused Randver to hang, and tread Svanhild under horse hooves. And when this was discovered by Gudrun, then she spoke to her sons.

1 Then I heard a quarrel of
a terribly violent sort,
reluctant words, spoken
out of great anguish,
when the hard-hearted one
whetted to battle
with grim words
Gudrun's sons.

2 Why sit,
why sleep through life?
Why aren't you grieving
as you speak of glad things?
When Jormunrekk
your sister,
young of life,
trod under horses,
white and black
on the army-road,
gray, tame of gait,
Gothic horses.

3 You are not like
Gunnar and them,
nor of the spirit
as Hogni was;
her would you
have endeavored to avenge,
if you had the mood
of my brothers
or the hard spirit
of the Hunnish kings.

4 Then said this Hamdir,
the stouthearted one:
Little did you
praise Hogni's deeds,
when they awakened Sigurd
from sleep;
your embroidery was,
the blue and white ones,
red in the husband's blood,
drenched in blood of the slain.

5 Was your
brother's vengeance
terrible and bitter,
when you murdered your sons;
all of us could have
on Jormunrekk,
of one mind,
avenged our sister.

6 Bring forth the treasure
of the Hunnish kings!
You have whetted us
to the sword-Thing.

7 Laughing Gudrun
went to the storehouse,
the mark of kings
out of chests chose,
long mail tunics,
and brought to her sons;
bravely loaded

123

onto the back of horses.

8 Then said this Hamdir,
the stouthearted one:
So comes back again,
to visit his mother,
spear-Niord, sank down
among Gothic people,
so you at the funeral feast
can drink for us all,
to Svanhild
and your sons.

9 Grieving Gudrun,
Giuki's daughter,
she went sorrowfully
to sit on the walkway,
and to tell
teary-cheeked,
moody spells
in many ways.

10 Three fires I knew,
three hearths I knew,
I was to three husbands
brought home;
alone was Sigurd to me
best of all,
whom my brothers
were the bane of.

11 A heavier wound
I have not seen nor known,
more they thought
to cause me harm,
when me the princes
gave to Atli.

12 The keen Hun
I called to me for a secret,
I could not for misfortune
have compensation,
before I cut the heads
from the Hniflungs.

13 I went to the shore,
I was angry at the Norns,
wanted to push away
their strife for peace;
lifted me, did not drown,
the high waves,
thus I climbed on shore,
so that I should live.

14 I went to bed

—did not seem better for me—
a third time
to the people's-king;
I begat children,
inheritance-guards,
Jonak's sons.

15 But with Svanhild
sat bondwomen,
of my children I
gave her the best of my love;
so was Svanhild
in my hall,
the same as the honorable
sun's beam.

16 I provided gold
and costly weaving,
before I gave her
to Gothic people;
that was the hardest
sorrow of mine
when the white
hair of Svanhild
was trod in the mud
under the hooves of horses.

17 But the most painful,
when they my Sigurd
robbed of victory,
in our bed;
and the grimmest
when they Gunnar,
glittering worm,
slithered to his vital flesh;
and the sharpest,
when to the heart
of the king not-a-coward
cut the quickened one.

18 I remember many misfortunes.
Fasten the bit, Sigurd,
on the black mare,
the horse quick to travel,
let it run hither!
Does not sit here
a daughter-in-law nor a daughter,
who to Gudrun
gave treasures.

19 You recall, Sigurd,
what we spoke of,
when we were together in bed
both of us agreeing,
that you would me,

moody one, visit,
hale, from Hel,
and I to you from the world.

20 Load up, jarls,
a pile of oak-wood,
let this be under heaven
the highest!
May burn the breast
full of evil the fire,

from around the heart
melt away sorrows.

21 All the jarls'
inheritances are better,
all the women's
sorrows are less,
this series of grief
has been told.

# The Ancient Lay of Hamdir

*Hamðismál in forno*

1 Sprung on the walkway
grievous deeds,
causing elves to weep
joy-hindered
early in the morning
men's wickedness
every anxiety
quickening sorrow.

2 That was not now
nor of yore,
a long time
has passed since then,
few are so old
that this was twice as far,
when whet Gudrun,
Giuki's child,
her young sons
to avenge Svanhild.

3 Your sister was
called Svanhild,
she whom Jormunrekk
trod under horses,
white and black
on the army-road,
gray, tame of spirit
Gothic horses.

4 You were pushed back,
kings of the people,
you alone live of
my family line.

5 I am standing alone
as an aspen on the hill,
kinsmen have fallen
as twigs from a fir,
destitute for joy
as wood for leaves,
when one damaging branches
comes on a warm day.

6 Then said this Hamdir,
the stouthearted one:
little did you then, Gudrun,
praise Hogni's deeds
when they Sigurd
awakened from sleep,
you sat on the bed,
and the killers laughed.

7 Your embroidery was,
the blue-white one,
woven by craftsmen,
flowing in your husband's blood.
When Sigurd died,
you sat over the dead one,
you showed no glee,
Gunnar wanted it so for you.

8 Atli you thought to injure
with Erp's murder
and with Eitil's life-loss,
but that was worse for you;
so should every other person
cause life-loss
with a sore-biting sword,
so that they do not cause pain.

9 Then Sorli said this
—he had wise insight:
I do not want to with mother
exchange words;
words are thought to be lacking
by both of you two:
what do you now ask, Gudrun,
that you grieve for not obtaining?

10 You grieve for your brothers
and sweet sons,
near-born kinsmen,
led near discord;
and you shall for us, Gudrun,
both grieve,

we here sitting fey on mares,
far away we will die.

11 Journeyed out of the courtyard,
howling with rage,
moved then over, the young men,
damp mountains,
on Hun mares,
to avenge the murder.

12 Found on the street
one capable of great things:
How will the short-brown one
help us?

13 The one born of a different mother
said he would give
help to kinsmen,
as one foot does to the other.
In what may a foot
help a foot,
or a flesh-grown
hand the other?

14 Then Erp said this
one time
—gloriously played
on the mare's back:
It is ill to a weaker man
show the road.
Said very harsh
the bastard was.

15 Drew out of their sheaths
the sheath-iron,
sword edges,
to delight the vile-woman;
caused their strength to diminish
a third,
let the young man
sink to the earth.

16 Shook their cloaks,
fastened on short swords,
and the god-descendants
put on costly-wear.

17 Ahead of them lay roads,
found the path to woe
and their sister's son
wounded on a tree,
the wind-cold wolf-tree
west of the farmstead;
the crane-whetter always moving,
it was not pleasant to linger there.

18 Loud merriment was in the hall,
men ale-cheerful,
and the Goths were not
to be heard
before a valiant man
sounded on a horn.

19 Went to say
to Jormunrekk,
that were seen
warriors under helms:
Deliberate on a plan!
Mighty ones are coming,
mighty men has the
maid who was trod.

20 Then Jormunrekk laughed,
he touched hand to beard,
asked for a fight,
battle-eager by wine;
he shook dark hair,
looked upon white shield,
he let his hand
twirl the gold cup.

21 Happy I then think myself
if I can see
Hamdir and Sorli
in my hall;
the boys I would then bind
with bow-strings,
the good sons of Giuki,
hang on a gallows.

22 Then Hrodrglod said this,
standing over the famous one,
the slender-fingered one spoke
with the man:
Because they called for
what they cannot obey;
may two men alone,
ten hundred Goths,
bind or battle
in the high fortress?

23 A stirring was in the house,
ale-cups fell down,
men lay in blood,
coming from the breasts of Goths.

24 Then said this Hamdir,
the stouthearted one:
You wished, Jormunrekk,
for us to come,
brothers of the same mother,

into your fortress.
You see your feet,
you see your hands,
Jormunrekk, thrown
in the hot fire.

25 Then roared
the divinely-descended one,
bold in his armor
as a bear roars:
Stone the men,
since the spears will not bite,
edges nor iron,
Jonak's sons.

26 Then said this Hamdir,
the stouthearted one:
Evil you brought about, brother,
when you loosened that bag,
often from that bag
comes baleful counsel.

27 You would have spirit, Hamdir,
if you had wisdom;
great are a man's wants,
if it is mother-wit.

28 Off the head would now be,
if Erp lived,

our brother was war-bold,
whom we killed on the road,
the man battle-bold
—the *dísir* whet me—
the man who shouldn't be fought
—they made me do it.

29 I do not think we will be
as the wolves' example,
to quarrel with ourselves,
like the Norns' dogs,
the greedy ones were
raised in the wilderness.

30 Well we have fought,
standing upon slain Goths,
over us, edge-weary,
is an eagle on a branch;
we have gotten good fame
though we die now or die in yore,
no man lives the evening
after the Norns' decree.

31 There fell Sorli
at the hall's gable,
and Hamdir sank
at the back of the house.

That is *The Ancient Lay of Hamdir*.

# The Hauksbok Völuspá

*Codex Arnamagnaeanus 544, also known as Hauksbok, is a collection of various Norse sagas. It also contains within its pages an alternate version of the Völva's Prophecy (Völuspá). Its insertion into the manuscript is somewhat of an enigma, as it was not written by Hauk Erlendson or either of his two scribes. It may have been penned, in fact, by the scribe responsible for Codex Arnamagnaeanus 242, "Codex Wormianus" of the Younger Edda. Evidently, an unknown scholar recognized its importance and placed it where it would not be lost. The Hauksbok Völuspá is far from perfect, but it contains elements not found within the Elder Edda, some of which are quite significant differences which correct errors in the Elder Edda. It is presented here in its entirety.*

1 I ask for the hearing of all
the holy kindred
greater and lesser
sons of Heimdall;
Valfadir wishes that I
properly tell
the ancient tales of men,
which are earliest remembered.

2 I remember the Jotuns
born in the early days
those who long ago
had nurtured me;
I remember nine worlds
nine wood-dwellers
the glorious Measure-tree
underneath the earth.

3 It was the earliest time
when Ymir lived
there was no sand nor sea
nor cool waves;
earth was not to be found
nor the upper heavens
Ginnungar was gaping
but no grass.

4 Then Bur's sons
raised it up
they who glorious
Midgard shaped;
the sun shone from the south
upon the hall of stone

then the ground was growing
green leaks.

5 The sun was in the south
the moon's companion
her best hand
over the rim;
the sun did not know
where she had a hall,
the stars did not know
where they had homesteads,
the moon did not know
what *megin* he possessed.

6 Then all the Powers went
to Rokstola,
the most holy gods,
and on this gave counsel:
night and the moon-phases,
names were given to them,
morning was named
and midday,
afternoon and evening,
to count the years.

7 The Aesir met
at Idavoll,
tested strengths,
put everyone to the test,
established forges,
smithed treasures,
shaped tongs
and made tools.

8 Played *tafl* in the courtyard,
they were cheerful,
they had no
want for gold;
until three came,
*thurs* daughters,
very powerful,
from Jotunheimar.

9 Then all the Powers went
to Rokstola,
the most holy gods,
and on this gave counsel:
how should the dwarven
lords be shaped
out of Brimir's blood
and from Blain's limbs.

10 There was Modsognir,
who was greatest
of all dwarves,
and Durin another;
they were formed like men,
many were made,
dwarves, out of the earth
as Durin said.

11 Nyi, Nidi,
Nordri, Sudri,
Austri, Vestri,
Althiof, Dvalin,
Naar and Nain
Niping, Dain,
Vegg, Gandalf,
Vindalf, Thorin;

12 Bifur, Bafur
Bombur, Nori,
An and Onar,
Ai, Miodvitnir,
Thrar and Thrain,
Thror, Lit, and Vit,
Nyr and Nyrad,
the dwarves I have now,
Regin and Radsvid,
rightly tallied.

13 Fili, Kili,
Fundin, Nali,
Hefti, Fili,
Hanar and Svid,
Nar and Nain,
Niping, Dain,
Billing, Bruni,
Bild and Buri,

Fror, Fornbori,
Freg and Loni;

14 Aurvang, Iari,
Eikinskialdi,
now  are told the dwarves
in Dvalin's company
the kinsmen
tallied with Lofar
those who went
to homes in muddy fields
at Jorovellir.

15 There was Draufnir,
and Dolgthraser,
Har, Haugspori,
Hlevarg, Gloin,
Skirfir, Virvir,
Skafid, Ai,
Alf and Yngvi,
Eikinskialdi.

16 They will be remembered
while men live
the long list of descendents
that Lofar had.

17 Until three came
mighty brothers
strong and loving
Aesir to the homestead;
found on the land
capable of little
Ask and Embla
*ørlög*-less;
souls they did not have
thoughts they did not have
with no vitality
nor healthy look.

18 Odin gave them souls
Hoenir gave thoughts
Lodur gave vitality
and healthy look.

19 I know an ash that stands
named Yggdrasil
the highest of trees dripping
white mud
thence comes the dew
that falls in the valley
the evergreen stands
over Urd's well.

20 Then came the women

very learned
three from the hall
that is near the tree;
Urd is one named
another Verdandi
carved wood slips
Skuld the third.

21 They lay fate
they determine lives
for the children of men
to declare ørlög.

22 Then all the Powers went
to Rokstola
the most holy gods
and on this gave counsel:
who had in the air
stirred mischief
and to the Jotun race
gave Od's girl.

23 Thor alone did battle
full of anger
he seldom sits
when he hears such things
that oaths were tread upon
words and promises
all the binding words
that between them had passed.

24 She knows Heimdall's
hearing is hidden
under the light-accustomed
holy tree
and she sees pouring down
a muddy waterfall
from the pledge of Valfadir—
do you know more, and what?

25 In the east lives and old woman
in Jarnvid
and there gives birth to
the kindred of Fenrir
out of all of them
a certain one
will devour the moon
in a troll's likeness;
26 flesh falls
from doomed men
the seats of the Powers are reddened
with red blood
black is the sunshine
the summer after
all weather is hostile—

do you know more, and what?

27 She remembers the troop-slaying
first in the world
when Gullveig
was supported by spears
and in Har's hall
she was burned
thrice burned
thrice born
often not seldom
though she still lives.

28 Heid they called her
when she came to their homes
and the *völva* revealed fate
with her wands;
she did *seidr* wherever she could
she did *seidr* in a trance
she was always a delight
to evil women.

29 Then all the Powers went
to Rokstola,
the most holy gods,
and on this gave counsel:
whether the Aesir should
pay tribute
or should all the gods
have the offerings.

30 Odin threw out
and shot into the troops
that was the troop-slaying
first in the world;
broken was the shield-wall
fortress of the Aesir
the Vanir used a battle-spell
to tread the valley.

31 Then vigorously Vali
twisted slaughter-bonds
rather strongly made
bonds from intestines;
there sits Sigyn
about her companion not at all
she was happy—
do you know more, and what?

32 Garm bays loudly
before Gnipahellir
the fetters will break
and the ravenous one runs;
I see from far away
I can tell much

131

all the way to Ragnarok
the mighty gods of battle.

33 Sitting there on a burial mound
and plucking a harp
the herdsman of *gygr*
glad Eggdir;
crowing over
the bird-wood
the fair red rooster
who is called Fialar.

34 Crowing over the Aesir
is Gullinkambi
to wake up the men
at Heriafadir's;
and another is loud
under the earth
a dirty red rooster
in the halls of Hel.

35 She sees a hall standing
far from the sun
at Nastrond
the door facing north;
drops of poison fall
in through the smoke-hole
the hall is braided
of serpents' backs.

36 She sees wading there
in the strong current
men who perjured
and murder-wolves
and those who seduced another's
confidant;
there Niddhogg sucks
corpses of those who pass on
shredding the wolfish ones—
do you know more, and what?

37 Now Garm bays loudly
before Gnipahellir
the fetters will break
and the ravenous one runs;
I see from far away
I can tell much
all the way to Ragnarok
the mighty gods of battle.

38 Brothers will fight
and until each is dead
the children of sisters will
spoil their bonds of trust;
it is hard in the world

much adultery
battle-age, short-sword age,
shields are split.

39 Wind-age, wolf-age,
before the world falls;
earth screams
witches fly
man will not
spare another's life.

40 Mim's sons play
and the Measurer burns
near the old
Giallarhorn;
loudly blows Heimdall
the horn is taken up
Odin speaks
with Mimir's head.

41 Yggdrasil shakes
the towering tree
the old tree groans
the Jotun is loose;
everyone is frightened
on the Hel-way
before Surt's
intimate engulfs it.

42 How is it with the Aesir
how is it with the elves?
All of Jotunheimar roars
the Aesir are at the Thing;
dwarves groan
before stone doors
the kings of the stone walls—
do you know more, and what?

43 Now Garm bays loudly
before Gnipahellir
the fetters will break
and the ravenous one runs;
I see from far away
I can tell much
all the way to Ragnarok
the mighty gods of battle.

44 Hrym comes from the east
holding a shield before him
Jormungand writhes
with Jotun-rage;
the serpent is splashing
and the eagle is screaming
cutting corpses with a pale beak
Naglfar is free.

45 A keel fares from the east
coming close are Muspel's
people on the waters
and Loki steers;
the monstrous sons are coming
all with the ravenous one
they are with the brother of
Byleist on the voyage.

46 Surt fares from the south
with the wood's enemy
shining on the sword is
the sun of the gods-of-the-slain;
the rocky cliff crashes down
greedy women stumble
men tread the Hel-way
and the heavens are burst asunder.

47 Then came the great
son of Sigfadir
Vidar striking
at the slaughter beast;
he came to Hvedrung's son
caused to stand
a sword in the heart
then his father was avenged.

48 Now Garm bays loudly
before Gnipahellir
the fetters will break
and the ravenous one runs;
I see from far away
I can tell much
all the way to Ragnarok
the mighty gods of battle.

49 Yawning high in the air
earth's girdle
the fearful gaping jaws
of the serpent in the air;
Odin's son will
meet the serpent
after the wolf dies
and Vidar's ...

50 [the text is illegible]

51 ... turns black
earth sinks into the mist
no longer crossing the heavens
are the bright shining stars;
raging steam
yokes the life-nourisher
tall flames play

against heaven itself.

52 Garm bays loudly
before Gnipahellir
the fetters will break
and the ravenous one runs;
I see from far away
I can tell much
all the way to Ragnarok
the mighty gods of battle.

53 She sees coming up
another time
earth from the sea
growing green;
the waterfall flows
the eagle flies over
that mountain
hunting for fish.

54 The Aesir meet
at Idavoll
and about the earth-encircling rope
mighty they discuss;
and they remember
the mighty events
and Fimbultyr's
ancient runes.

55 Then will Aesir
the wondrous
golden *tafl*-pieces
find in the grass
those that they in days of old
had owned.

56 Unsown will
the fields grow
all misfortune will be set right
Balder will come;
Hod and Balder live together
at Hropt's site of victory
the gods-of-the-slain are well—
do you know more, and what?

57 Then may Hoenir
choose lot-twigs
and dwell the sons
of two brothers
in wide Vindheim—
do you know more, and what?

58 She sees a hall standing
fairer than the sun
thatched in gold

133

at Gimle;
there shall trustworthy
people dwell
and will through all ages
enjoy bliss.

59 Then comes the Power
to rule the gods
strong from above
that rules all.

60 Comes the dark
dragon flying
the glittering adder beneath
from Nida;
clearly seen on the wings
flying over the field
of Nidhogg are dead bodies—
now she must sink.

# The Waking of Angantyr

*The Waking of Angantyr is found within the Saga of Hervor and King Heidrek, contained in the Hauksbok manuscript and in Codex Regius 2845. It was surely once part of a longer cycle of poems similar to the heroic lays of the Elder Edda, but these no longer survive.*

*Tyrfing was a sword forged by dwarves who laid three special enchantments upon it: its wounds never heal, it will bring death to its owner, and it will bring about three infamous deeds. Angantyr Arngrimsson had possession of Tyrfing when he died in a duel with Hialmar. Though victorious, Hialmar was wounded in the battle and died by Tyrfing's edge. The sword was subsequently buried with Angantyr on the isle of Samsey. Angantyr's daughter was born shortly thereafter. When she matured, Hervor was filled with the need to avenge her father. She traveled to Samsey to claim Tyrfing as her own, her thirst for revenge outweighing any fears of the undead or of the blade's sinister enchantment.*

1 The young maiden met
in Munarvag
at sunset
a man with a herd.

The herder said:
2 Who is this one
who comes to the island?
You should go quickly
to night lodgings.

Hervor said:
3 I will not go
to night lodgings
because I do not know
this island's inhabitants;
quickly tell,
before leaving here,
where is Hiorvard's
mound known to be?

The herder said:
4 Do not ask about this,
it is not wise,
leader of Vikings
you are in dire straits;
let us depart as swiftly
as our feet can go,

far away
from this loathsome place.

Hervor said:
5 I offer treasures to you
to pay for the information,
this noble one is not
easy to dissuade;
of no use to me are
handsome ornaments
or fair rings,
so I will not keep them.

The herder said:
6 It seems foolish to me
to journey there
on our own
as the shadows grow long;
a fire is more suitable
than an open mound,
the earth and bogs burn—
run away quickly!

Hervor said:
7 Let us not be afraid
of such blustering
even though the whole island
burns with flame;

135

let us not by
dead warriors
be trembled,
we shall talk to them.

8 The herder went then
hastily to the forest,
far from speech
with the maid;
but the hard-knit
heart in her breast
by such things
was swelled in Hervor.

She saw the burning mounds and the
mounds' inhabitants roaming outside,
but went to the mounds and was not
afraid; she passed through the flames
as if they were smoke until she came
to the mound of the berserker. Then
she spoke:

9 Awaken, Angantyr!
Hervor awakens you,
the only daughter
of yours by Tofa;
release from the mound
the sharp sword
that Svafrlami
the dwarf forged.

10 Hervard, Hiorvard,
Hrani, Angantyr!
Awaken, all of you
under the tree roots,
helmeted and armored,
swords sharpened,
with shields and gear,
spears bloodied.

11 The reports are numerous,
sons of Arngrim,
that violent kinsmen
increase on the earth;
should not
the sons of Eyfura
speak with me
at Munarvag?

12 You all can see
inside the ribs
of yourselves are bugs,
wasted in the mounds
unless the sword is released
which Dvalin hammered,

to honor the dead
reveal the precious weapon.

Then Angantyr answered:
13 Daughter Hervor
why do you speak such
terrible words?
This will go badly for you!
Insane is the request,
you are out of your wits
and deluded
to awaken dead men!

14 My grave wasn't dug
by my father or friends,
but they had Tyrfing
the two who lived,
although it was possessed
by only one afterwards.

She said:
15 Speak the truth!
The Aesir laid you
whole in the mound
and you had possession
of Tyrfing with you!
You hesitate to give
the inheritance
to your only child.

Then a great fire appeared over the
mound as it stood opened. Then said
Angantyr:

16 The Hel-gates are open,
the mounds are agape,
all is aflame
on the island you can see;
it is terrible outside
to gaze upon.
You do not realize, maiden,
what may be shaped for you!

She said:
17 Burns not
the night fires
such that by flames I
would be frightened from you.
It will not tremble, the maid's
heart in her breast,
although she sees spirits
sitting in the doorways.

Then Angantyr said:
18 I ask you, Hervor,

for your attention,
wise daughter,
to what will be:
Tyrfing will be,
if you trust in its might,
to your family, maiden,
always destructive.

19 You will get a son
that will afterwards
bear Tyrfing
and trust in its strength;
then Heidrek will
be called by people
the greatest of all
under the sun's canopy.

She said:
20 I cast a spell
on dead men
those who would
all lay
dead with the ghosts
rattling in the graves:
Deliver, Angantyr,
from the mound
what dwarves smithed,
what you try to conceal.

He said:
21 Do not summon, young maid,
the men's corpses
to you from the mound
stroll this night,
with inlaid spears
and Gothic metal
helmeted and armored
before the hillside's entrance.

22 I thought the men
human until this,
before your hall
I sought after;
release from the mound
the breaker of armor,
cleaver of shields,
and bane of Hialmar.

Angantyr said:
23 Lying under my shoulder
is Hialmar's bane,
it is completely
engulfed in flames;
I do not know a maid
anywhere on earth

that would dare this sword
take into hand.

She said:
24 I would keep it
and take it in hand,
the sharp sword
if I could;
I do not fear
the fiery brand,
the flames will diminish
when I gaze upon it.

He said:
25 It is foolish, Hervor,
to have such mindset
that you would open-eyed
rush into the flames;
yet I will release
the sword from the mound
to the young maiden.
I cannot refuse.

She said:
26 You do well,
Viking kinsman,
when you give to me
the sword from the mound;
it now seems better to me,
Budlung, to have,
than to obtain
all of Norway.

He said:
27 You do not know—
wretched are these words,
deceitful woman—
when to rejoice;
Tyrfing will thus,
if trust is given to it,
your family, maiden,
completely destroy.

She said:
28 I will go
to the sea steed,
the king's maid is now
in good spirits;
I am little afraid of that,
buried king,
how my sons
will afterwards contend.

He said:
29 You shall not have it

and enjoy it for long,
keep in the sheath
Hialmar's bane,
touch not the edges—
poison is on both—
this measurer of man
is harmful.

30 Fare well, daughter,
I readily give you
twelve men's lives,
if taken with trust--
the strength and endurance,
all that was good,
that the sons of Arngrim
lost in death.

She said:
31 All you dwell—
the road urges me—
safely in the mound!
I will quickly depart.
I'll feel most
at home when
there surrounds me
burning flames.

# EIRIK'S LAY

*Eirik's Lay is found in the Fagrskinna manuscripts: Codices Arnamagnaeanus 51, 52, 301, and 302. All of these are copies of originals which are now lost. The first stanza is also quoted in the Younger Edda.*

*Eirik Bloodaxe was in line to inherit the throne of Norway after his father, Harald Fairhair, died in the mid-tenth century. The kingdom was denied him, however, when he was challenged by his brother, Hakon the Good. Eirik fled Norway and sought for a dominion of his own in England. He was crowned king of York within a couple of years, but he was quickly expelled by his subjects. Four years later, he regained the throne, but was driven out again two years afterwards. Soon thereafter, he perished at the battle of Stainmore.*

*Eirik was survived by his much celebrated wife, Gunnhild, and five sons who were destined to be kings. Gunnhild was a remarkable woman, and her support of her sons earned her the moniker Mother of Kings. One of her finest achievements was the commissioning of a poem in honor of her late husband. Curiously, although Eirik and Gunnhild were most assuredly Christian, the lay follows the Odinic Tradition.*

Odin said:
1 What's that I dreamt?
  I thought I rose at daybreak
  to prepare Valholl
  for slain warriors;
  I awakened the *einheriar*,
  bid them to rise up,
  to strew benches,
  to wash beer mugs;
  Valkyries brought wine
  because a king was coming.

2 To the homestead I
  expect a hero comes,
  one of distinction
  who gladdens my heart.
  What thunder is this, Bragi,
  as if a thousand marching
  or a great army?

Bragi said:
3 The benches all break
  as if Balder comes
  up to Odin's hall.

Odin said:
4 Such foolish words

should not come from wise Bragi,
because you know well what it is:
the clamor is Eirik
as he is coming,
a king to Odin's hall.

5 Sigmund and Sinfiotli,
  rise at once
  and go to meet the king;
  you should ask
  Eirik to come in,
  I have been expecting him.

Sigmund asked:
6 Why do you expect Eirik,
  rather than another?

Odin said:
7 Because often among men
  he has reddened blades
  and bloodied swords.

Bragi asked:
8 Then why did you deny him victory
  if you feel he is so glorious?

Odin said:

139

9 Because it is uncertain to know
when the gray wolf
comes to the god's home.

Sigmund said:

10 Hail now, Eirik,
you are welcome to enter
and come to the hall, wise one.

I want to know
who accompanies you,
as kings from a great battle.

Eirik answered:

11 There are five kings,
they are all known by name,
and I myself am the sixth.

# Balder's Dreams

*Codex Arnamagnaeanus 748 contains fragments of both the Elder and Younger Eddas. Of particular interest is that it also contains the only surviving copy of Balder's Dreams.*

*The style of Balder's Dreams is very similar to the Völva's Prophecy. The poem utilizes the motif of Odin seeking out wisdom from a dead völva.*

1 At once the Aesir went
all to the Thing,
and the Asynior,
all to deliberate;
and on this debated
the mighty gods:
why were Balder's
dreams baleful?

2 Up rose Odin,
men's sacrifice,
and he on Sleipnir
laid a saddle;
he rode downward thence
to Niflhel,
he met a whelp there
coming out of Hel.

3 There was blood
on the front of its breast
and at *galdr's* father
it barked a long time;
Odin rode further,
the fold-way thundered,
he came to the high
house of Hel.

4 Then Odin rode
before the eastern door,
where he knew
a *völva* lay;
over the prophetic one he
spoke *galdr* for the dead
until reluctantly rising,
she spoke these words:

5 Who is this man,
unknown to me,

who has caused me
an arduous journey?
I was snowed upon
and wet by rain
and dew soaked;
dead I was a long time.

6 Vegtam I am called,
the son I am of Valtam,
tell me about Hel,
I know about home;
for whom are the benches
strewn with rings,
the bench places beautifully
flooded in gold?

7 Here stands for Balder
brewed mead,
shining drink,
shields hang overhead,
and the sons of the Aesir
are in suspense;
reluctantly I said this,
now I will stay silent.

8 Don't you stay silent, *völva*,
I want to question you
until I know all,
and I want to know this:
who will Balder's
bane be
and Odin's son
rob of life?

9 Hod will send the high
glorious twig thence,
he will Balder's
bane be

141

and Odin's son
rob of life;
reluctantly I said this,
now I will stay silent.

10 Don't you stay silent, *völva*,
I want to question you
until I know all,
and I want to know this:
who will avenge Hod's
hateful deed
and Balder's killer
carry to the pyre?

11 Rind gives birth
in the western hall
so that Odin's son
may fight one night old,
hands unwashed,
head unkempt,
until to the pyre is carried
Balder's opposition;
reluctantly I said this,
now I will stay silent.

12 Don't you stay silent, *völva*,

I want to question you
until I know all,
and I want to know this:
who are the maids
that will mourn
and to heaven throw
their neck-flaps?

13 You are not Vegtam
as I thought,
rather you are Odin
the old sacrifice!

You are not a *völva*
nor a wise woman,
rather you are the mother
of three *thursar*!

14 You ride home, Odin,
and be proud of victory,
but none will come
afterwards to visit
until Loki loosens
limbs from bonds
and Ragnarok
comes with destruction.

# Hyndla's Song

*Hyndla's Song is found in the Flateyiarbok, Codex Regius 1005. Stanza 33 is also found in the Younger Edda, where it is stated as coming from "The Volva's Shorter Prophecy"; most scholars generally feel that stanzas 29 through 44 come from this otherwise lost poem.*

*Ottar must prove his ancestry in order to claim his inheritance against Angantyr. Freyia, his patron, disguises him as her boar and rides him to the home of Hyndla, a wise Jotun well versed in ancient lore.*

1 Awake, maiden of maidens,
awake, my friend,
sister Hyndla
who lives in a cave,
now is the darkest of darkness,
we shall ride
to Valholl
and to the holy sanctuary.

2 Ask Heriafadir
to sit in good spirits,
he rewards and gives
gold to the worthy;
he gave Hermod
a helm and mail shirt,
and Sigmund
received a sword.

3 He gives victory to some
and some gain treasures,
eloquence to many,
and mother-wit to men;
fair winds he gives to men,
and poetry to scalds,
he gives manliness
to many warriors.

4 To Thor she will sacrifice,
this she will request:
that he always with you
shows favor,
although he is infrequently so
with Jotun women.

5 Now take your wolf

from the stall,
let him run
with my wild boar.
Slow is your gelding
treading the god-way,
it will not my steed,
most excellent, overcome.

6 You are deceitful, Freyia,
when you put me to the test,
when your eyes look
at me that way,
when you have with you
on the path of the slain,
Ottar the young,
Innstein's son.

7 You deceive yourself, Hyndla,
I think you are dreaming
when you speak of my companion
on the path of the slain;
here is my golden boar,
the gold-bristled
Hildisvini,
he was made by a skillful
pair of dwarves,
Dain and Nabbi.

8 Let us quarrel out of our saddles,
we should sit
and about the boar's
lineage debate,
these men
who are descended from gods.

143

9 They have wagered
Welsh metal,
Ottar the young
and Angantyr;
it is fitting to help
so that the young warrior
may have the father-leavings
from his kinsmen.

10 He made an altar to me
laden with stones,
now those rocks
are glass;
he reddens it anew
with cow's blood,
Ottar is always trusted
among the Asynior.

11 Now you let the ancient
kinsmen be told,
and the children of
the man's family:
who are the Skioldungs,
who are the Skilfings,
who are the Odlings,
who are the Ylfings,
who are freeman-born,
who are chieftain-born,
the chosen men
of Midgard?

12 You are Ottar,
born to Innstein,
and Innstein was
of Alf the Old,
Alf was of Ulf,
Ulf of Saefari,
and Saefari
of Svan the Red.

13 Your father had a mother
made stately by necklaces,
I think that she was named
Hledis the Priestess,
Frodi was her father
and Friaut her mother,
all their family is considered
among the superior ones.

14 Ali was once
strongest of men,
before Halfdan
highest of the Skioldungs;
renowned were the troop-slayings
that made them valorous,

his deeds were well thought of
between heaven's corners.

15 He was strengthened with Eymund,
noblest of men,
and he struck Sigtrygg
with cold edges;
went on to take Almveig,
noblest of women,
they had and raised
eighteen sons.

16 Thence came the Skioldungs,
thence came the Skilfings,
thence the Odlings,
thence the Ynglings,
thence the freeman-born,
thence the chieftain-born,
the most chosen men
in Midgard;
all are your family,
Ottar the Homish.

17 Hildigun was
your mother,
born to Svava
and Saekonung;
all are your family,
Ottar the Homish,
it is important to know this,
will you go further?

18 Dag had Thora,
mother of warriors,
their family raised
the noblest champions:
Fradmar and Gyrd
and both Frekis,
Am and Josurmar,
Alf the Old;
it is important to know this,
will you go further?

19 Ketil was called their friend,
Klypp's inheritor,
he was the mother's father
of your mother;
from them came Frodi
before Kari,
the eldest was
gotten by Alf.

20 Nanna was the next,
Nokkvi's daughter,
her son was

144

your father's in-law,
forgotten is that kinship,
I will tell further back;
I knew both Brodd and Horvir,
all are your family,
Ottar the Homish.

21 Isolf and Asolf
sons of Olmod
and Skurhildar,
Skekkil's daughter,
you should tally
many warriors,
all are your family,
Ottar the Homish.

22 Gunnar Wall-divider,
Grim Word-scratcher,
Thorir Ironshield
Ulf Yawner.

23 Bui and Brami,
Barri and Reifnir,
Tind and Tyrfing,
and the two Haddingi,
all are your family,
Ottar the Homish.

24 Ani, Omi,
were born
sons of Arngrim
and Eyfura;
noisy berserkers
evils of many kinds,
on land and on sea,
going along like flame,
all are your family,
Ottar the Homish.

25 I knew both
Brodd and Horvir,
they were in the court
of Hrolf the Old,
all born
from Jormunrekk,
Sigmund's in-laws—
hear my saga—
a grim warrior,
the woe of Fafnir.

26 The prince was
from the Volsungs,
and Hiordis
from Hraudung,
but Eylimi

was from the Odlings,
all are your family,
Ottar the Homish.

27 Gunnar and Hogni,
Giuki's heirs,
and also Gudrun,
their sister;
Guthorm was not
of Giuki's family,
although he was brother
to both of them,
all are your family,
Ottar the Homish.

28 Harald Battle-tooth,
born of Hroerek,
slinger-of-rings;
he was Aud's son,
Aud Deep-riches
was Ivar's daughter,
and Radbard was
Randver's father;
they were men
consecrated by the gods,
all are your family,
Ottar the Homish.

29 Eleven were
the Aesir counted,
Balder was laying
on the deathbed;
for this Vali
came to avenge
his brother;
he struck the killer.

30 Balder's father was
Bur's inheritor;
Frey had Gerdi,
she was daughter to Gymir,
of the Jotun race,
and Aurboda,
and Thiazi was
their kinsman,
the shoot-eager Jotun,
Skadi was his daughter.

31 Much we have said to you,
and will more,
what I feel should be known;
do you want more?

32 Haki was Hvaedna's
best son by far,

145

and Hvaedna had
Hiorvard as father,
Heid and Hrossthiof
were the children of Hrimnir.

33 All *völva* are
from Vidolf,
all *vitki*
from Vilmeid,
and *seidr*-bearers
from Svarthofdi,
all Jotuns
come from Ymir.

34 Much we have said to you,
and will more,
what I feel should be known;
do you want more?

35 One was born
in days of old
fortified with much strength,
kin to the Powers;
nine gave birth to him,
the magnificent man,
Jotun maids
from the earth's edge.

36 Much we have said to you,
and will more,
what I feel should by known,
do you want more?

37 Gialp bore him,
Greip bore him,
bore him Eistla
and Eyrgiafa,
bore him Ulfrun
and Angeyia,
Imd and Átla
and Iarnsaxa.

38 He was fortified
by earth's *megin*,
the ice-cold sea
and the blood sacrifice.

39 Much we have said to you,
and will more,
what I feel should be known;
do you want more?

40 Loki sired the wolf
with Angrboda,
and got Sleipnir
with Svadilfari;
one witch is thought
most evil of all,
that which from the brother
of Byleist came.

41 Loki ate of the heart
burned on linden-wood,
he took it half charred,
the woman's heart stone;
Lopt was impregnated
by the evil woman,
thence on the earth
comes every wicked woman.

42 The sea storms
against heaven itself,
passes over the land,
and the air fails;
then will come snow
and mighty winds,
thus it is ordained
that the Powers will end.

43 One was born
greater than all,
he was empowered
with the earth's *megin*;
of peacemakers he is said to be
the wealthiest,
bound in peace
to the all-mighty ones.

44 Then comes another
powerful one,
though I dare not
name him;
few now see
further along,
when Odin will
meet the wolf.

45 Bring the memory ale
to my boar,
so he will completely
recollect the words
of this conversation
on the third morning,
when he and Angantyr
reckon their ancestries.

46 Turn away from here,
I long for sleep,
you got from me few
fair choices;

you leapt, noble friend,
out into the night,
as with the goats
Heidrun goes.

47 You ran to Od
always yearning,
several have thrust
under your fore-shirt;
you leapt, noble friend,
out into the night,
as with the goats
Heidrun goes.

48 I laid a fire
over the wood-dwellers,
so that you could not
come away from here.

49 A fire I see burning,
the earth all aflame,
it would be most
life-threatening to suffer;
carry to Ottar
a beer to hand,
blended with much poison,
a curse of ill fortune!

50 Your curse words shall
have no strength,
although you, Jotun woman,
call down evil;
he shall drink
the precious drink,
I bid Ottar
all good in the test.

# BIBLIOGRAPHY

*Edda: Die Lieder des Codex Regius nebst verwandten Denkmalern.* Hrsg. von Gustav Neckel. Band I. Text. 4. umgearbeitate Auflage von Hans Kuhn. Heidelberg: Carl Winter Universitätsverlag, 1983.

*Glossary to the Poetic Edda Based on Hans Kuhn's Kurzes Worterbuch.* Beatrice La Farge and John Tucker. Heidelberg: Carl Winter Universitätsverlag, 1992.

*A Concise Dictionary of Old Icelandic.* Geir T. Zöega. Oxford at the Clarendon Press, 1910.

# GLOSSARY

**dís** (plural **dísir**) supernatural feminine beings who influence the destiny and luck of specific individuals and/or families.

**dísir** *see* **dís**

**einheri** (plural *einheriar*) "single-combatant," the heroes who dwell in Valholl, each of whom is hand-picked by Odin's valkyries. They will fight alongside the gods at Ragnarok.

**einheriar** *see* **einheri**

**fylgia** a supernatural being attached to an individual or family; a fetch. A fylgia often allows itself to be seen when death is imminent, thus *fylgia* are often considered harbingers of death.

**galdr** a type of magic associated with the use of runes and chants.

**gýgr** a monstrous woman, an ogress.

**hamingia** a supernatural being of protection.

**knörr** a merchant ship and cargo vessel of the Viking age, similar in design to a longship, but with a deeper draft and wider beam.

**megin** strength, especially the supernatural power of gods. Also, an individual's inner strength.

**Naud** "need," a rune, having the phonetic value equal to "n."

**ørlög** the progression of fate through the accumulation of cause and effect relationships

**rastir** *see* **röst**

**ríst** to cut, carve, or scratch, especially in reference to runes.

**röst** (plural rastir) a unit of distance, literally from one rest to another, approximately 4 to 5 miles.

**seidr** a magic distinctive for its use of trances and prophecy.

**strandhögg** the practice of re-supplying ships through raiding. It was made illegal by most rulers, but this did little to discourage the practice against foreign countries.

**tafl** also called hnefitafl. A game played during the Viking age, rules unknown. It has two types of pieces: the king and pawns.

**thurs** (plural thursar) an alternate term for Jotun, used especially in reference to particularly violent individuals.

**Thurs** a rune, having the phonetic value equal to "th."

**thursar** *see* **thurs**

**vitki** term used to refer to a man well versed in ancient lore, wisdom, and magic.

**völva** term used to denote a woman well versed in lore and prophecy.

# JNDEX

The index contains all proper names, Old Norse terms, and other special words found within the text. An attempt has been made to provide many of these names with a literal translation. These should not be considered definitive as many are based upon conjecture. Entries are referenced by the abbreviated poem titles and stanza numbers.

**Aegir** (Sea) a Jotun, the personification of the ocean itself; Grim 45; Hymr 1,39; Loki intro,3-4,10,14,16,18,27,65; 1 Helgi 29

**Aegishiálm** see *Oegishiálm*

**Aesir** the primary race of gods, especially the males; Volva 7,16,24-25,29,42,49,57; Havi 143,159-160; Vafd 28,38,50; Grim 4,6,29-30,37,42,44-45; Skir 7,17-18,33-34; Harb 25; Hymr 2,31; Loki intro,2-3,6,8,10 prose-13,19,25,27,30-31,33,35,37,53,56,64,end prose; Thrym 2,7,13-15,17; Alvis 10,16,26,34; Regin intro, 5 prose; Fafn 13-14; Sigrd 4,18; Atli 27; Hauk 7,17,29,30,34,42,54,55; Waking 15; Balder 1,7; Hyndla 29

**Agnar** Sigrd 4 prose

**Agnar Geirrodsson** Grim intro,2,3,end prose

**Agnar Hraudungsson** Grim intro

**Ai** (Great-grandfather) a dwarf; Volva 11; Hauk 12

**Aldafadir** (Old-father) Odin; Vafd 4,53

**Aldarrok** (Doom-of-life) a term for the end times, probably identical to Ragnarok; Vafd 39

**Alf¹** (Elf) a dwarf, this dwarf's name has been seen to be an indicator of relationship between the dwarven and elven races; Volva 15; Hauk 15

**Alf²** Hyndla 19

**Alf Dagsson** Hyndla 18

**Alf Hialprecsson** Sinf 3¶

**Alf Hrodmarsson** Hior 34 prose,39

**Alf Hundingsson** 1 Helgi 14; 2 Helgi 13 prose

**Alf Ulfsson** Hyndla 12

**Alf the old** 1 Helgi 52

**Alfadir** (All-father) Odin; Grim 48; 1 Helgi 38

**Alfheim** (Elf-home) the dwelling place of the "light" elves; Grim 5

**Alfhild** (Elf-warrior) Hiorvard's wife; Hior intro

**Alfrodul** (Elf-beam) the sun; Vafd 47

**Algroen** (All-green) an island; Harb 16

**Ali** Hyndla 14

**Allvaldi** (All-ruler) a Jotun, Thiazi's father; Harb 19

**Almveig** Hyndla 15

**Alof** Hior intro,5 prose

**Alsvid** (All-burning) one of the horses that draw the sun across the sky; Grim 37

**Althiof** (All-thief) a dwarf; Volva 11; Hauk 11

**Alvis** (All-knowing) a dwarf; Alvis 3,9,11,13,15,17,19,21,23,25,27,29,31,33

**Alvit** (All-wise) a swan-maiden; Volun intro

**Am** Hyndla 18

**An** (Loved one) a dwarf; Volva 11; Hauk 12

**Anar** (Laborer) a dwarf; Volva 11

**Andhrimnir** Grim 18

**Andvari** (Furless) a dwarf; Regin intro-4 prose,5 prose; Nifl 2¶

**Angantyr**[1] Waking 9,10,13,15 prose,18,20

**Angantyr**[2] Hyndla 9

**Angantyr**[3] Hyndla 45

**Angeyia** a Jotun; Hyndla 37

**Angrboda** a Jotun; Hyndla 40

**Ani** Hyndla 24

**Arastein** (Eagle-stone) an unknown location, probably a mountain; 1 Helgi 14; 2 Helgi 13 prose

**Arngrim**[1] Waking 11,30

**Arngrim**[2] Hyndla 24

**Arvak** (Early-waker) one of the two horses that draws the sun across the sky; Grim 37; Sigrd 15

**Asa-Thor** (Thor-of-the-Aesir) Thor; Harb 52

**Asgard** (Aesir's-Enclosure) the home of the Aesir; Hymr 7; Thrym 9,18

**Ask** (Ash) the first human man; Volva 16; Hauk 17

**Asmund** (A-god's-bride price) Grim 49

**Asolf** Hyndla 21

**Asvid** (God-tree) a Jotun; Havi 143

**Asynior** the females of the primary race of gods; Loki 31; Thrym 14; Sigrd 4; Balder 1; Hyndla 10

**Atla** a Jotun; Hyndla 37

**Atli Budlisson** (Fierce) character based upon the historical Attila the Hun; Frag 5; 1 Gud 25; Short 32-33,36,40,56,58-60; Nifl 1¶-3¶; 2 Gud 26,37; 3 Gud intro-1,10; Odd intro,2,20-25,30-31; Atli intro,1,3,14,16,26,30,33-36,39,41,end prose; Green 2,4,19-20,40-48,55,59,66-67,71,73,77-78,86-87,95,98,102; Whet 11; Hamd 8

**Atli Hringsson** 1 Helgi 52

**Atli Idmundsson** Hior intro,2-3,4 prose,5 prose,11 prose,13,15,19-20,22,30

**Atrid** (Mover) Odin; Grim 48

**Bolverk** Odin; Havi 109; Grim 47

**Bombur** dwarf; Volva 11; Hauk 12

**Borghild** (Fierce-mountain) 1 Helgi 1; 2 Helgi intro; Sinf 1¶,3¶

**Borgny** Odd intro,4-5,7

**Borgunds** Atli 18

**Bragalund** 2 Helgi 8

**Bragi** one of the Aesir; Grim 44; Loki intro,8,12-16; Sigrd 15; Eirik 2-4,8

**Bragi Hognisson** 2 Helgi 20, 29 prose

**Bralund** (Brow-grove) Helgi Hundingsbane's home; 1 Helgi 1,3; 2 Helgi intro

**Brami** Hyndla 23

**Brandey** an island; 1 Helgi 22

**Bravoll** 1 Helgi 42

**Breidablik** (Broad-white) Grim 12

**Brimir**[1] Ymir; Volva 9; Hauk 9

**Brimir**[2] (Surf) Aegir; Volva 36

**Brimir**[3] (Sword) a sword; Sigrd 14

**Brisingamen** (Necklace of the Brisings) Freyia's necklace; Thrym 13,15,19

**Brodd** Hyndla 20,25

**Brunavagar** (Torrid-bay) 2 Helgi 4 prose-6

**Bruni** a dwarf; Hauk 13

**Brynhild** (War-Hild) Grip 27,35,45; Frag 3,8,10,14; 1 Gud 22-23,25,27,end prose; Short 3,15,19,27,30; Bryn intro,4-5; 2 Gud 27; Odd 15-18

**Budli** Grip 27; Frag 8,14; 1 Gud 23,25,27; Short 15,30,56,70; Bryn 4; 2 Gud 26-27; 3 Gud 1; Green 36,53,61,74,88,94

**Budlung** (Descendant of Budli, figurative) a kenning for "prince"; 1 Helgi 12,56; Hior 2,39,40,43; 2 Helgi 30,44; Waking 26

**Budlungs** (Descendants of Budli, literally) 1 Helgi 2; Hior 3; Atli 43

**Bui** Hyndla 23

**Bur** (Son) Odin's father; Volva 4 ; Hauk 3; Hyndla 30

**Buri** a dwarf; Hauk 13

**Byggvir** (Barley) Loki intro,43,45,46

**Byleist** Loki's brother; Volva 48; Hauk 45; Hyndla 40

**Dag**[1] (Day) Vafd 25; Sigrd 3

**Dag**[2] Hyndla 18

**Dag Hognisson** 2 Helgi 23 prose,29 prose,34

**Dain**[1] (Excellent-one) an elf; Havi 143

**Dain**[2] a hart; Grim 33

**Dain**[3] a dwarf; Hauk 11,13; Hyndla 7

**Danparstadir** (Chief's Homestead) Atli 5

**Delling** Havi 160; Vafd 25

**Denmark** Sinf 3¶; 1 Gud end prose; 2 Gud 14

**dís** (plural dísir) Grim 53; 1 Helgi 16; Regin 24; Sigrd 9; 1 Gud 19; Atli 36; Green 26; Hamd 28

**dísir** see **dís**

**Dogling** (Descendant of Dag) kenning for "prince"; 1 Helgi 7,16,26

**Dolgthraser** a dwarf; Hauk 15

**Dolgthrasir** (Hostile-talker) a dwarf; Volva 15

**Draufnir** a dwarf; Hauk 15

**Draupnir** (Dripper) dwarf; Volva 15

**Duneyr** (Rusher) a hart; Grim 33

**Durathror** a hart; Grim 33

**Durin** dwarf; Volva 10; Hauk 10

**Dvalin**[1] (Delayed) dwarf; Volva 14; Havi 143; Alvis 16; Fafn 13; Hauk 11,14; Waking 12

**Dvalin**[2] a hart; Grim 33

**dwarf** (dwarves, dwarven) a supernatural race of creatures known for their coarse looks, subterranean habitat, and skill as smiths and miners; Volva 9-10,12,14,49; Havi 143,160; Alvis 9,11-17,19,21-27,29-31,33,35; Regin intro; Hauk 9,10,12,14,42; Waking 9,20; Hyndla 7

**Eggdir** Hauk 33

**Eggther** Volva 41

**Egill**[1] a Jotun; Hymr 7

**Egill**[2] Volund's brother; Volun intro,2,4

**Eikthyrnir** a hart; Grim 26

**Eikin** (Oaken) a river; Grim 27

**Eikinskialdi** (Oaken Shield) a dwarf; Volva 13; Hauk 14,15

**einheriar** (Single-combatants) Vafd 41; Grim 18,24,36,51; Loki 60; 1 Helgi 38; Eirik 1

**Eirik Bloodaxe** Eirik 4-6,10,11

**Eistla** a Jotun; Hyndla 37

**Eitil** Atli's son; Nifl 1¶; Atli 38; Hamd 8

**Eitrdal** (Venom-dale) Volva 36

**Eldhrimnir** (Sooty-cauldron) Grim 18

**Eldir** Loki intro-1,2,4,5

**elf** (elves, elven) a supernatural race of creatures known for their beauty and magic; Volva 49; Havi 143,160; Grim 4; Skir 4,7,17-18; Loki intro,13,30; Thrym 7; Volun 10,13,32; Alvis 10,12,14,16,18,20,22,24,28,30,32; Fafn 13; Sigrd 18; Hamd 1; Hauk 42

**Elivagar** (Birth-sea) Vafd 31; Hymr 5

**Embla** the first human woman; Volva 16; Hauk 17

**Erp**[1] Atli's son; Nifl 1¶; Atli 38; Hamd 8

**Erp²** Jonak's son; Whet intro; Hamd 14,28

**Eyfura¹** Hyndla 24

**Eyfura²** Waking 11

**Eyiolf** 1 Helgi 14; 2 Helgi 13 prose

**Eylimi** Hior 9 prose,30 prose; Sinf 3¶; Grip intro,9; Regin 15; Hyndla 26

**Eymod** 2 Gud 19

**Eymund** Hyndla 15

**Eyrgiafa** Hyndla 37

**Fafnir** a man transformed into a serpentine beast; Grip 11,13; Regin 9 prose,11 prose,12,14 prose; Fafn intro,1,8,12,14,21-23,26-28,31 prose,32,38,39 prose,end prose; 1 Gud intro; Bryn 10; Nifl 1¶; Odd 17; Hyndla 25

**Falhofnir** (Falling-hooves) a horse; Grim 30

**Farmatyr** (Tyr of Cargoes) Odin; Grim 48

**Feng** (Snatcher) Odin; Regin 18

**Fenrir** a wolf, monstrous offspring of Loki; Volva 39; Vafd 46-47; Loki 38; 1 Helgi 40; Hauk 25

**Fensalir** Volva 34

**Fialar¹** a dwarf; Volva 15; Harb 26; Hauk 33

**Fialar²** a hen; Volva 41

**Fialar the wise** Havi 14

**Fili** a dwarf; Volva 13; Hauk 13

**Fimafeng** (Nimble-carrier) Loki intro

**Fimbulthul** (Great-rhapsody) a river; Grim 27

**Fimbultyr** (Great-Tyr) Odin; Volva 57; Hauk 54

**Fimbulvetr** (Great Winter) the three-year long winter that precedes Ragnarok; Vafd 44

**Finn** (Finder) a dwarf; Volva 15

**Finnar** an ancient tribe; Volun intro

**Fiolnir** Odin; Grim 47; Regin 18

**Fiolsvid** (Very-wise) Odin; Grim 47

**Fiolvar** (Very-aware) Harb 16

**Fiorgyn** (Life-eager) Jord; Volva 53; Harb 56

**Fiorgynn** Frigg's father; Loki 26

**Fiorm** a river; Grim 27

**Fiornir** Atli 10

**Fiorsungs** 2 Helgi 25

**Fioturlund** (Fetter-grove) 2 Helgi 23 prose,30

**Fitiung** Havi 78

**Fivi** 2 Gud 16

**Folkvang** (Warrior's Field) Freyia's hall; Grim 14

**Gerd** Skir 10 prose,19,39,41

**Geri** one of Odin's personal wolves; Grim 19

**Giaflaug** (Chasm-flyer) 1 Gud 4

**Giallarhorn** (Resounding-horn) Heimdall's horn; Volva 45; Hauk 40

**Gialp** a Jotun; Hyndla 37

**Gimle** Volva 61; Hauk 58

**Ginnar** (Fool) a dwarf; Volva 15

**Ginnungar** a poetic play upon the word Ginnungagap, the emptiness that pre-
dated everything; Volva 3; Hauk 3

**Giol** a river; Grim 28

**Gipul** a river; Grim 27

**Gisl** (Warder) a horse; Grim 30

**Giukungs** (Descendants of Giuki) Short 35; Nifl 1¶,3¶

**Giuki** Gunn's father; Grip 13-14,31,43,47,50; Fafn 41; Frag 6,9,11,end prose;
1 Gud 4,12,16-18,20,24; Short 1-2,30; Bryn 4-5,13; 2 Gud 1-2,38; 3 Gud 2;
Odd intro,21,28,end prose; Atli intro-1; Green 1,48,50,103; Whet 9; Hamd
2,21; Hyndla 27

**Giuki Hognisson** Nifl 3¶

**Glad** (Glad) a horse; Grim 30

**Gladsheim** (Glad-home) Grim 8

**Glaer** (Glistening) a horse; Grim 30

**Glapsvid** (Tree-enticer) Odin; Grim 47

**Glasislund** Hior 1

**Glaum** (Noisy Cheer) a horse; Atli 29

**Glaumvor** (Merry-sounding) Nifl 3¶; Green 6,21,30

**Glitnir** (Glittering) Forseti's hall; Grim 15

**Gloi** (Glowing) a dwarf; Volva 15

**Gloin** a dwarf; Hauk 15

**Gnipahellir** (Summit-cavern) Volva 43,46,55; Hauk 32,37,43,48,52

**Gnipalund** (Summit-land) 1 Helgi 30,34,40,50

**Gnitaheid** (Gnita Heath) site of Fafnir's lair; Grip 11; Regin 14 prose; Atli 5

**Godthiod** (Godly-people) Volva 31

**Goin** a serpent; Grim 34

**Gol** (Screamer) a valkyrie; Grim 36

**Gomul** (Old) a river; Grim 27

**Gondlir** (Sorcerer) Odin; Grim 49

**Gondul** a valkyrie; Volva 31

**Gopul** a river; Grim 27

**Goths** Grim 2; Grip 35; Frag 9; Bryn 8; Gud 17; Atli 8,20; Whet 2,8,16; Hamd
3,18,22-23,30; Waking 21

**Habrok** (Hawk) Grim 44

**Haddingi** Hyndla 23

**Haddingiar** (Blond-haired) 2 Gud 22

**Haeming** 2 Helgi intro-1

**Hagal** 2 Helgi intro-2

**Haki** Hyndla 32

**Hakon** 1 Gud end prose; 2 Gud 14

**Half** 2 Gud 13

**Halfdan** (Half-Dane) 2 Helgi end prose; Hyndla 14

**Hamal** 2 Helgi 1,6

**Hamdir** Whet intro,4,8; Hamd 6,21,24,26-27,31,end prose

**hamingia** Vafd 49

**Hamund** Sinf 1¶

**Hanar** a dwarf; Volva 13; Hauk 13

**Har¹** (Hairy) a dwarf; Volva 15; Hauk 15

**Har²** (High) Odin; Volva 21; Grim 46; Hauk 27

**Harald Battle-tooth** Hyndla 28

**Harbard** (Hairy-beard) Odin; Grim 49; Harb 10,15,19,23,27,29,39,51

**Hatafiord** (Hata-fjord) Hior 11 prose

**Hati¹** (Hated) a Jotun; Hior 11 prose,24

**Hati²** a wolf; Grim 39

**Hatun** (High-place) 1 Helgi 8,25

**Haugspori** (Cairn-dweller) a dwarf; Alvis 15; Hauk 15

**Havard** (High-cairn) Hunding's son; 1 Helgi 14

**Havi** (High-one) Odin; Havi 111,164

**Hedin** (Fur-jacket) Hiorvard's son; Hior intro,30-34 prose,41

**Hedinsey** (Hedin's Isle) 1 Helgi 22

**Hefti** a dwarf; Hauk 13

**Heid¹** Volva 23; Hauk 28

**Heid²** Hyndla 32

**Heiddraupnir** (Bright-dripper) Sigrd 13

**Heidrek¹** Odd intro-1

**Heidrek²** Waking 19

**Heidrun** (Bright-rune) Grim 25; Hyndla 46,47

**Heimdall** (Home-dale) one of the Aesir, the watchman of Bilrost; Volva 1,28,45; Grim 13; Loki 47,48; Thrym 15; Hauk 1,24,40

**Heimir** Grip 19,27-29,31,39

**Hel¹** daughter of Loki, mistress of the underworld; Volva 42; Grim 31; Fafn 21,39; Bryn 8; Green 53-54; Hauk 34; Balder 3

**Hel²** the underworld realm of the dead ruled by Hel¹; Volva 50; Vafd 43; Grim

28; Skir 27; Harb 27; Loki 63; Alvis 14,18,20,26,32,34; Hior 29; Fafn 10,34; 1 Gud 8; Bryn intro; Green 39,41,49,95; Whet 19; Hauk 41,46; Waking 16; Balder 2,6

**Helblindi** (Hel-blind) Odin; Grim 46

**Helgi Haddingiascadi** Helgi Hundingsbane reborn; 2 Helgi end prose

**Helgi Hiorvardsson** Hior 6-7,9 prose,10,11 prose,13,17,24,26,29,30 prose,31,34,38,42,end prose; 2 Helgi intro

**Helgi Hundingsbane** 1 Helgi intro,1,8,18,23,29,50,53; 2 Helgi intro-1 prose,4-4 prose,10,13-14,18 prose,19 prose,23 prose,25,31,33,37-39,42,44-45,47,49 prose,end prose; Sinf 1¶; Grip 15

**Hepti** (Haft) a dwarf; Volva 13

**Herborg** 1 Gud 6

**Herfiotur** (Troop-fetter) a valkyrie; Grim 36

**Herfadir** (Troop-father) Odin; Volva 30

**Heriafadir** (Harry-father) Odin; Volva 42, Vafd 2; Grim 19,25-26; Hauk 34; Hyndla 2

**Herian** (Harrier) Odin; Volva 31; Grim 46; 1 Gud 19

**Herkia** 3 Gud intro,10-11

**Hermod** Hyndla 1

**Herteit** Odin; Grim 47

**Hervard¹** Hunding's son; 2 Helgi 13 prose

**Hervard²** Waking 10

**Hervor¹** Volun intro,15

**Hervor²** Waking 3,5,7,8,13,18,25

**Hialli** (Chatterer) Atli 22-23,25; Green 59

**Hialm-Gunnar** (Helm-Gunnar) Sigrd 4 prose; Bryn 8

**Hialmar** Waking 23,29

**Hialmberi** (Helmet-bearer) Odin; Grim 46

**Hialprek** Sinf 3¶; Regin intro,15 prose; Fafn intro

**Hild** (Warrior) a valkyrie; Volva 31; Grim 36; 2 Helgi 23

**Hildigun** Hyndla 17

**Hildisvini** Hyndla 7

**Hild-under-the-helm** Brynhild; Bryn 7

**Hildolf** Harb 8

**Himinbiorg** (Heavenly-rock) Heimdall's home; Grim 13

**Himinfiol** (Heavenly-mountain) 1 Helgi 1

**Himinvangar** (Heavenly-fields) Helgi's estates; 1 Helgi 8,15

**Hindarfial** (Hindar's Falls) Fafn 42; Sigrd intro

**Hiordis** Sigmund's wife; Sinf 3¶; Grip intro; Hyndla 26

**Hiorleif** 1 Helgi 23

**Hiorvard**[1] Helgi's father; Hior intro,1,3,5 prose,10,11 prose,30 prose,38

**Hiorvard**[2] a Jotun; Hyndla 32

**Hiorvard**[3] Waking 3,10

**Hiorvard Hundingsson** 1 Helgi 14; 2 Helgi 13 prose

**Hladgud** Volun intro,15

**Hlebard** (Shelter-beard) a Jotun; Harb 20

**Hlebiorg** (Shelter-hill) 2 Helgi 21

**Hledis** Hyndla 13

**Hlesey** (Shelter-isle) Laesso; Harb 37; 2 Helgi 6; Odd 29

**Hlevang** a dwarf; Volva 15

**Hlevarg** a dwarf; Hauk 15

**Hlidskialf** Odin's high seat; Grim intro; Skir intro

**Hlin** Volva 51

**Hlodvard** Hior 19

**Hlodver** Volun intro,10,15; 2 Gud 25

**Hlodyn** lord; Volva 53

**Hlok** (Screamer) a valkyrie; Grim 36

**Hlorridi** (Trembling-hot) Thor; Hymr 4,16,27,29,37; Thrym 8,14,31

**Hlymdalir** (Noisy Dales) Brynhild's home; Bryn 7

**Hniflung** (Niflung) Hogni's son; Green 86

**Hniflungs** (Niflungs) 1 Helgi 48; Whet 12

**Hnikar** (Pusher) Odin; Grim 47; Regin 18-20

**Hnikud** Odin; Grim 48

**Hod** the blind god, one of the Aesir, slayer of Balder; Volva 33,59; Hauk 56; Balder 9,10

**Hodbrodd** Granmar's son; 1 Helgi 18,35,48; 2 Helgi 13 prose,16,19,25-26,29 prose

**Hoddmimir** (Mimir-of-the-treasure-hoard) Vafd 45

**Hoddrofnir** (Treasure-hoard-breaker) Sigrd 13

**Hoenir** one of the Aesir; Volva 17,60; Regin intro; Hauk 18,57

**Hogni**[1] Giuki's son; Grip 37,50; Frag 7; Short 14,17,44-45; Nifl 1¶,3¶; 2 Gud 7,9-10,19,31; 3 Gud 8; Odd 8,27; Atli 6,12,19,21,23-26; Green 6-7,10-11,13-14,28,33,36,38,57-59,6 2-63,69,87,89; Whet 3-4; Hamd 6; Hyndla 27

**Hogni**[2] Sigrun's father; 1 Helgi 17,52,56; 2 Helgi 4,13 prose,17-18,20,23 prose,29 prose

**Hol** (Sloped) a river; Grim 27

**Hornbori** (Horn-bearer) a dwarf; Volva 13

**Horvir** Hyndla 20,25

**Hraesvelg** (Very-dreadful) a Jotun, origin of the wind; Vafd 37

**Hrani** Waking 10

**Hraudung** Grim intro; Hyndla 26

**Hreidgotar** (Hreid-Goths) Vafd 12

**Hreidmar** Regin intro,5-11 prose

**Hrid** a river; Grim 28

**Hrimfaxi** (Rime-mane) the horse that draws the night; Vafd 14

**Hrimgerd** a Jotun; Hior 17-29

**Hrimgrimnir** Skir 35

**Hrimnir** (Rime-covered) a Jotun; Skir 28; Hyndla 32

**Hring** (Ring) 1 Helgi 52

**Hringstadir** (Ringed Homesteads) Helgi's estates, 1 Helgi 8, 1 Helgi 56

**Hringstod** (Ringed Homesteads) Helgi's estate, 1 Helgi 8

**Hrist** a valkyrie; Grim 36

**Hrod** (Infamous) a Jotun; Hymr 11

**Hrodmar** Hior 5 prose,11,34 prose

**Hrodrglod** Hamd 22

**Hrodrsvitnir** (Infamous-wolf) Fenrir; Loki 39

**Hrodvitnir** (Infamous-wolf) Fenrir?; Grim 39

**Hroerek** Hyndla 28

**Hrolf** Hyndla 25

**Hrollaug** (Shiver-bath) 2 Helgi 21

**Hron** a river; Grim 28

**Hroptatyr** (Invoker-Tyr) Odin; Havi 160, Grim 54

**Hropt** (Invoker) Odin; Volva 59; Grim 8; Loki 45; Sigrd 13; Hauk 56

**Hrossthiof** Hyndla 32

**Hrotti** (Rough) a sword; Fafn end prose

**Hrungnir**, a Jotun, Harb 14-15; Hymr 16; Loki 61,63

**Hrym** (Decrepit) a Jotun; Volva 47; Hauk 44

**Hugin** (Thought) one of Odin's ravens; Grim 20; 1 Helgi 54; Regin 18,26; Fafn 35; 2 Gud 29

**Humlung** Hior intro

**Hunaland** (Land of the Huns) 1 Gud 6; Odd 4

**Hunding** 1 Helgi 10,11,14,53; 2 Helgi 1,4 prose,10,13 prose,39; Sinf 3¶; Grip 9; Regin 15, conclusion

**Hundland** (Hunding's Land) 2 Helgi intro

**Hunmork** (Hun-mark) Atli 13

**Huns** 2 Gud 15; Atli 2,4,12,15-16,27,34,38; Whet 3,6,12

**Hvaedna** Hyndla 32

**Hvedrung** Loki; Volva 52; Hauk 47

**Hvergelmir** (Screaming Hot Springs) the source of rivers; Grim 26

**Hymir** a Jotun; Hymr 5,7,10-11,15,21,25,29,30,35,39; Loki 34

**Hymling** Hiorvard's son; Hior intro

**Hyndla** a Jotun; Hyndla intro,1,7

**Iari** a dwarf; Volva 13; Hauk 14

**Iarnsaxa** a Jotun; Hyndla 37

**Idavoll** (Eddy-dale) Volva 7,57; Hauk 7,54

**Idmund** Hior intro,2

**Idunn** one of the Asynior; Loki intro,16-18

**Ifing** a river; Vafd 16

**Imd** a Jotun; 1 Helgi 43; Hyndla 37

**Im** a Jotun; Vafd 5

**Inguna-Frey** Frey; Loki 43

**Innstein** Hyndla 6,12

**Isolf** Hyndla 21

**Isung** 1 Helgi 20

**Ivaldi** a dwarf; Grim 43

**Ivar** Hyndla 28

**Jafnhar** (Even-high) Odin; Grim 49

**Jalk** Odin; Grim 49,54

**Jarizkar** 2 Gud 19

**Jarizleif** 2 Gud 19

**Jarnvid** (Iron-wood) Volva 39; Hauk 25

**Jonak** Short 62-63; Whet intro,14; Hamd 25

**Jord** (Earth) a Jotun, the personification of the Earth; Loki 58; Thrym 1

**Jormungand** (Immense-wand) the serpent that encircles the world, the Midgard's Serpent; Volva 47; Hauk 44

**Jormunrekk** Short 64; Whet intro,2,5; Hamd 3,19,20,24; Hyndla 25

**Jorovellir** (Stallion-vales) Volva 14; Hauk 14

**Josurmar** Hyndla 18

**Jotun** an ancient race of gigantic creatures noted for their ferocity and knowledge; Volva 2,26,36,45,47; Havi 104,106,108,143,164; Vafd 1-2,4-6,8,15-16,19-21,30,32-35,37,42; Grim 11,50; Skir 8,25,30,34; Harb 15,19-20,23; Hymr 3,9,12-14,17,20,25,28,30; Thrym 18,22-24,26,28-29,31-32; Alvis 10,12,14,16,18,20,22,24,26,28,30,32,34; Hior 17,25; Fafn 29,38; Hauk 2,41,44; Hyndla 4,30,33,35,50

**Jotunheimar** (Jotun-homes) the realm of the Jotuns; Volva 8,49; Skir intro,10 prose,40; Thrym 5,7,9,13,21,26,28; Hauk 8,42

**Kara** 2 Helgi end prose

**Kara's Song** a lost poem; 2 Helgi end prose

**Kari** Hyndla 19

**Kerlaug** the name of two rivers; Grim 29

2 Gud 21; Hauk 5; Hyndla 38,43

**Meili** Harb 9

**Melnir** (Bit-champ) a horse; 1 Helgi 51

**Menia** (Keepsake) a Jotun; Short 52

**Midgard** (Middle-enclosure) the world of man; Earth; Volva 4,53; Grim 41; Harb 23; Hauk 3; Hyndla 11,16

**Midvidnir** a Jotun; Grim 50

**Mim** a Jotun, Mimir; Volva 45; Sigrd 14; Hauk 40

**Mimir** a Jotun; Volva 29; (spear-Mimir) 1 Helgi 14; Hauk 40

**Miodvitnir** a dwarf; Volva 11; Hauk 12

**Miollnir** Thor's hammer; Vafd 51; Hymr 36; Loki 57,59,61,63; Thrym 30

**Miskorblinda** (Blended-with-malice) Hymr 2

**Mist** a valkyrie; Grim 36; 1 Helgi 47

**Modi** (Wrath) Thor's son; Vafd 51; Hymr 34

**Modsognir** a dwarf; Hauk 10

**Mogthrasir** a Jotun; Vafd 49

**Moin** (Moor-dweller) a serpent; Grim 34

**Moinsheimar** (Moor-homes) 1 Helgi 46; 2 Helgi 29

**Mornaland** (Morning Land) Odd 1

**Motsognir** a dwarf; Volva 10

**Munarvag** Waking 1,11

**Mundilfoeri** father of the sun and moon; Vafd 23

**Munin** (Memory) one of Odin's ravens; Grim 20

**Muspel** Volva 48; Loki 42; Hauk 45

**Mylnir** a horse; 1 Helgi 51

**Myrkheim** (Mirk-home) Atli 43

**Myrkvid** (Mirk wood) the Black Forest; Loki 42; Volun 1; 1 Helgi 51; Atli 3,5,13

**Naar** a dwarf; Hauk 11,13

**Nabbi** a dwarf; Hyndla 7

**Naglfar** (Nail-ship) a ship made from the nails of corpses; Volva 47; Hauk 44

**Nagrind** (Corpse-gate) Loki 63

**Nain** a dwarf; Hauk 11,13

**Nali** (Needle) a dwarf; Volva 13; Hauk 13

**Nanna** Hyndla 20

**Nar** (Corpse) a dwarf; Volva 12; Hauk 13

**Narfi** Loki's son, a wolf; Loki end prose

**Nari** Loki's son; Loki end prose

**Nastrond** (Corpse-shore) Volva 37; Hauk 35

**Naud** Sigrd 7

**Ofnir²** a serpent; Grim 34

**Ogn** (Dread) 1 Helgi 21; Fafn 42

**Oin** a dwarf; Regin 2

**Okolnir** Volva 36

**Olmod** Hyndla 21

**Olrun** (Ale-rune) Volun intro,4,15

**Omi¹** (Sounder) Odin; Grim 49

**Omi²** Hyndla 24

**Ominnis** (Forgetfulness) a heron; Havi 13

**Onar** a dwarf; Hauk 12

**Orkning** Green 28

**ørlög** Volva 16,20; Havi 56; Loki 21,25,29; Volun 1,3; 1 Helgi 3; Grip 28; Regin 14; Hauk 17,21

**Ormt** a river; Grim 29

**Orvasund** (Orva Sound) 1 Helgi 24

**Osci** (Wish) Odin; Grim 49

**Oskopnir** island where the Aesir will fight Surt's forces; Fafn 15

**Otr** (Otter) Regin intro,9 prose

**Ottar** Hyndla 6,9,10,12,16,17,20,21,23,24,26,27,28,49,50

**Power** Havi 80; Hauk 59

**Powers** (Old Norse: regin) the ruling gods, especially the Aesir; Volva 6,9,24,26,40; Havi 80,142; Vafd 3,13-14,25,39,44,46-48,50,52,54; Grim 4,6,37,41; Hymr 4; Loki 4,32,41; Alvis 10,20,30; Sigrd 19; Hauk 6,9,22,26,29; Hyndla 35,42

**Radbard** Hyndla 28

**Radgrid** a valkyrie; Grim 36

**Radseyiarsund** (Redseyiar's Sound) Harb 8

**Radsvid** (Wise Counselor) a dwarf; Volva 12; Hauk 12

**Raevil** Regin 16

**Ragnarok** (Doom of the gods) the destiny of many of the gods is to die in a great battle; Volva 43,46,55; Vafd 55; Loki 39; 2 Helgi 40; Green 22; Hauk 32,37,43,48,52; Balder 14

**Ran** 1 Helgi 30; Hior 18; Regin intro

**Randgrid** (Shield Peace) a valkyrie; Grim 36

**Randver** Whet intro; Hyndla 28

**rastir** see **röst**

**Ratatosk** (Traveling Tusk) a squirrel; Grim 32

**Regin** (Coward) a dwarf; Volva 12; Fafn 11; Regin intro,9 prose,11 prose,12 prose,13,14 prose,17,conclusion; Fafn intro,22-23,26 prose,29,33,37,39; Hauk 12

**Reginleif** a valkyrie; Grim 36

**Sigarsholm** (Sigar's Island) Hior 8

**Sigarsvellir** (Sigar's Vales) Helgi's land; 1 Helgi 8; Hior 34 prose-35

**Sigfadir** (Victory-father) Odin; Volva 52; Grim 48; Loki 58; Hauk 47

**Siggeir** (Victory-spear) Odin; 1 Helgi 41; 2 Gud 16

**Sigmund¹** Volsung's son; 1 Helgi 6,11; 2 Helgi intro,12,15,18 prose,50; Sinf 1¶-4¶; Grip 3; Regin 13; Fafn 4; Sigrd 1; Short 38; 2 Gud 16; Eirik 5,6,10; Hyndla 2

**Sigmund²** Sigurd's son; 2 Gud 28

**Sigrdrifa** (Victory Driver) Fafn 44; Sigrd 4 prose-5

**Sigrlin** Hior intro-1,4-5 prose,35

**Sigrun** (Victory-rune) 1 Helgi 30,54; 2 Helgi 4 prose,13 prose-14,18 prose-18,22-23 prose,49 prose,end prose

**Sigtrygg** Hyndla 15

**Sigtyr** (Victory-Tyr) Odin; Atli 30

**Sigurd** (Victorious) Sinf 3¶-4¶; Grip intro,3,5-6,8,10,16,19-20,24-26,30,36,40,43,52; Regin intro,12 prose,14 prose-15 prose,17,conclusion; Fafn intro,1 prose,4,20,22 prose,23,25,27,28,30,31 prose,32,39 prose,40,41,end prose; Sigrd intro-2 prose; Frag 2,5-8,11,end prose; 1 Gud intro-1,13,17-18,21-22,end prose; Short 1-3,6,8,11,13,21,63-65; Bryn intro,13-14; Nifl 1¶; 2 Gud 1-4,7-8,12,28-29; Odd 19; Green 96; Whet intro,10,17-19; Hamd 6-7; Hyndla 25

**Sigyn** Loki's wife; Volva 35; Loki end prose; Hauk 31

**Silfrintopp** (Silver Forelock) a horse; Grim 30

**Sindri** (Silvery-sparkle) a dwarf; Volva 36

**Sinfiotli** 1 Helgi 8,33,37,45; 2 Helgi 18 prose,25,28; Sinf 1¶; Eirik 5

**Sinir** a horse; Grim 30

**Sinriod** Hior intro

**Skadi** (Scathe) Grim 11; Skir intro; Loki intro,49,51,end prose; Hyndla 30

**Skafid** a dwarf; Volva 15; Hauk 15

**Skatalund** (Taxed Land) Bryn 9

**Skekkil** Hyndla 21

**Skeggiold** a valkyrie; Grim 36

**Skeidbrimir** (Surf-runner) a horse; Grim 30

**Skidbladnir** (Warship-cloth) a ship that can be folded up as a piece of cloth; Grim 44

**Skilfing** (Rightfully Gotten) Odin; Grim 54

**Skilfings** Hyndla 11,16

**Skinfaxi** (Shining Mane) a horse; Vafd 12

**Skioldungs** 2 Helgi 23-24,51; Fafn 44; Frag 14; Green 2; Hyndla 11,14,16

**Skirfir** a dwarf; Hauk 15

**Skirnir** (Baptized) Skir intro,2,10-10 prose,39 prose-40

**Svan the Red** Hyndla 12

**Svanhild** Short 55,63; Nifl 1¶; Whet intro, 8,15-16; Hamd 2-3

**Svanhvit** (Swan-white) Hladgud Svanhvit; Volun intro,2

**Svarang** (Sworn Grief) Harb 29

**Svarinshaug** (Oath-mound) 1 Helgi 31; 2 Helgi 13 prose

**Svarthofdi** Hyndla 33

**Svasud** Sumar's father; Vafd 27

**Svava**[1] Eylimi's daughter; Hior 9 prose,11 prose,30 prose,37,40-41,43,end prose

**Svava**[2] Hyndla 17

**Svavakonung** (King of the Svava) Hior 5 prose

**Svavaland** Hior 5 prose

**Sveggiud** a horse; 1 Helgi 47

**Svid** a dwarf; Hauk 13

**Svidiod** (Land of Sviar) Sweden; Volun intro

**Svidrir** (wise) Odin; Grim 50

**Svidur** (Singed) Odin; Grim 50

**Svipal** Odin; Grim 47

**Svipud** a horse; 1 Helgi 47

**Sviur** a dwarf; Volva 13

**Svol**[1] a river; Grim 27

**Svol**[2] the shield that protects Arvak and Alsvid from the heat of the sun; Grim 38

**Sylg** (Drink) a river; Grim 28

**tafl** Volva 8,58; Hauk 8,55

**Thakkrad** (Grateful Counselor) Volun 39

**Thekk**[1] (Well Liked) Odin; Grim 46

**Thekk**[2] a dwarf; Volva 12

**Thialfi** Harb 39

**Thiazi** a Jotun; Grim 11; Harb 19; Loki 51; Hyndla 30

**Thing** (Assembly) a formal legal gathering, "sword-Thing" and "armor-Thing" are kennings for battle; Volva 49; Havi 25,61,114; Grim 49; Skir 38; Hymr 39; 1 Helgi 29,50-51; 2 Helgi 50; Sigrd 5,12,24; Frag end prose; Short 27; 2 Gud 4; Green 99; Whet 6; Hauk 42; Balder 1

**Thiodnuma** a river; Grim 28

**Thiodrek** (Princely Man) 2 Gud intro; 3 Gud intro,2-3,5

**Thiodrorir** a dwarf; Havi 160

**Thiodvitnir** (Prince Wolf) Grim 21

**Thol** a river; Grim 27

**Tholley** Lodin's home; Hior 25

**Thor** one of the Aesir; Volva 27; Grim 4,29; Harb intro,9-18,22,24,26,28,32,36, 50,52,56; Hymr 23,28; Loki intro,56 prose,58-61,63; Thrym 9,15,17-19; Hauk 23; Hyndla 4

**Thora¹** 1 Gud end prose; 2 Gud 14

**Thora²** Hyndla 18

**Thorin** (Courageous) a dwarf; Volva 12; Hauk 11

**Thorir** Hyndla 22

**Thorsnes** (Thor's Ness) 1 Helgi 40

**Thrain** (Obstinate) a dwarf; Volva 12; Hauk 12

**Thrar** Hauk 12

**Thridi** (Third) Odin; Grim 46

**Thror¹** Odin; Grim 49

**Thror²** a dwarf; Volva 12; Hauk 12

**Thrudgelmir** a Jotun; Vafd 29

**Thrudheim** (Strength-Home) Thor's hall; Grim 4

**Thrud** (Strong) a valkyrie; Grim 36

**Thrym** (Stand-fast) a Jotun; Thrym 6-7,11,22,25,30-31

**Thrymheim** (Storm-home) Skadi's hall; Grim 11

**Thund¹** a river; Grim 21

**Thund²** Odin; Havi 145; Grim 46,54

**thurs** Volva 8; Havi 109; Vafd 33; Grim 31; Skir 30,34,35; Hymr 19; Thrym 6,11,18,22,25,30,31; Alvis 2; 1 Helgi 40; Hior 25; Hauk 8; Balder 13

**Thurs** Skir 36

**Thyn** (Thin) a river; Grim 27

**Tind** Hyndla 23

**Tofa** Waking 9

**Troney** 1 Helgi 24

**Tyr** one of the Aesir; Hymr 4,33; Loki intro,37-40; Sigrd 6

**Tyrfing¹** a sword; Waking 14,15,18,19,27

**Tyrfing²** Hyndla 23

**Ud** Odin; Grim 46

**Ulf** Hyndla 12,22

**Ulfdalir** (Wolf Dale) Volun intro,5-6,1 3

**Ulfrun** Hyndla 37

**Ulfsiar** (Wolf Lake) Volun intro

**Ull** one of the Aesir; Grim 5,42; Atli 30

**Unavagar** 1 Helgi 31

**Unn** (Wave) 2 Helgi 31

**Urd** (Wyrd) one of the three principle Norns; Volva 18-19; Havi 111; Hauk 19,20

**Vadgelmir** a river; Regin 4

**Vafdrudnir** (Strong Tangler) a Jotun; Vafd 1-3,6,20,22,24,26,28,30,32,34,36,38, 42

**Vafud** (Hanged) Odin; Grim 54

**Vak** (Watcher) Odin; Grim 54

**Valaskialf** a hall; Grim 6

**Valbiorg** (Rock of the Slain) 2 Gud 33

**Valdar** 2 Gud 19

**Valfadir** (Father of the Slain) Odin; Volva 1,28; Grim 48; Hauk 1,24

**Valgrind** (Gate of the Slain) Grim 22

**Valholl** (Hall of the Slain) Odin's hall where the einheriar reside; Volva 34; Grim 8,24; 2 Helgi 38 prose; Eirik 1; Hyndla 1

**Vali¹** Odin's son; Vafd 51; Hyndla 29

**Vali²** Loki's son; Hauk 31

**Valir** (foreigners) Short 66

**valkyrie(s)** (chooser-of-the-slain) feminine beings that choose the warriors for Valholl from among those who fall in battle; Volva 31; Volun intro; 1 Helgi 38; Hior 5 prose,9 prose,30 prose; 2 Helgi 4 prose,13 prose,18 prose,end prose; Sigrd 4 prose; Eirik 1

**Valland** Harb 24; Volun intro; Bryn 2

**Valtam** Balder 6

**Van** a river; Grim 28

**Vanaheim** (Vanir-home) Vafd 39

**Vandilsve** 2 Helgi 35

**Vanir** the secondary race of gods; Volva 25; Vafd 39; Skir 17-18,37; Thrym 15; Alvis 10,12,18,22,24,26,28,32,34; Sigrd 18; Hauk 30

**Var** (Spring) one of the Asynior; Thrym 30; Var of gold at Bryn 2 is a kenning for "woman"

**Varinsey** (Varin's Island) 1 Helgi 37

**Varinsiord** (Varin's Fjord) 1 Helgi 26

**Varinsvik** (Varin's Bay) Hior 22

**Vegg** Hauk 11

**Vegsvin** (Hard-way) a river; Grim 28

**Vegtam** Balder 6,13

**Vei** Loki 26

**Veig** (Strong-one) a dwarf; Volva 12

**Veor** (Guardian of the Sanctuary) Thor; Hymr 11,17,21

**Veratyr** (Tyr of Men) Odin; Grim 3

**Verdandi** one of the three principle Norns; Volva 19; Hauk 20

**Verland** Harb 56

**Ydalir** (Yew-dale) Ull's home; Grim 5

**Ygg** (Terrible) Odin; Vafd 5; Grim 53; Hymr 2; Fafn 43

**Yggdrasil** (Ygg's Steed) the World Tree; Volva 18,45; Grim 31-32,34-35,44; Hauk 19,41

**Yggiung** (Frightening One) Odin; Volva 29

**Ylfings** 1 Helgi 5,34,49; 2 Helgi intro,4,8,47; Hyndla 11

**Ylg** (She-wolf) a river; Grim 28

**Ymir** (Groaner) a Jotun; Volva 3; Vafd 21,28; Grim 40; Hauk 3; Hyndla 33

**Ynglings** Hyndla 16

**Yngvi**[1] a dwarf; Volva 15; Hauk 15

**Yngvi**[2] Frey; 1 Helgi 55; Regin 14

**Yngvi**[3] a man; 1 Helgi 52

# ORDER FORM

I would like to order my own or another copy of *The Elder Edda*. Please send me:

\# books x $19.95 per copy = _____

+ Postage (first class) & handling @ $4.95/book: _____

TOTAL ENCLOSED $ _____

We accept cash, check, or money order made out to Northbooks, or VISA, Mastercard. Prices subject to change without notice.

*(You may phone your VISA/MC order to Northbooks at 907-696-8973)*

VISA/MC card # ☐☐☐☐ ☐☐☐☐ ☐☐☐☐ ☐☐☐☐

Exp. date: \_\_\_\_/\_\_\_\_ Amount charged: $ _____

Signature: _____

Phone number: _____

Please send my book (s) to:

Name: _____

Address: _____

City: _____ State: _____ Zip: _____

Fill out this order form and send to:

## NORTHBOOKS
**17050 N. Eagle River Loop Rd, #3**
**Eagle River, AK 99577-7804**
**(907) 696-8973**
**www.northbooks.com**

LaVergne, TN USA
20 November 2009
164799LV00004B/7/P